Home Interiors

HOME INTERIORS
Edition 2007

Work Conception: Carles Broto
Publisher: Carles Broto
Editorial Coordinator: Jacobo Krauel
Graphic designer & production: Pilar Chueca, Oriol Vallès
Text: contributed by the architects,
edited by William George and Marta Rojals

© Carles Broto i Comerma
Jonqueres, 10, 1-5, Barcelona 08003, Spain
Tel.: +34 93 301 21 99   Fax: +34-93-301 00 21

info@linksbooks.net   ꓱ2ꟼ
www. linksbooks.net

Home Interiors

index

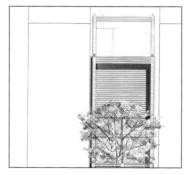

introduction

Interior design is one of the fields of architecture that has most evolved in recent decades. Dynamic new trends and changes are seen in the creative use of materials and in unprecedented construction styles. In response to increasingly discerning clients with a growing range of stipulations, architects working in interior design have been obliged to explore new fields, forging new paths and adapting them to the tastes of new generations. The challenge often lies in interpreting the demands of the client (who may be excessively steeped in passing fads or commercial needs) and, subsequently, in assigning a creative value to them. Thus, in all interior design one sees an effort to strike a balance between function and aesthetics, between the essential and the non-essential. On the following pages, you will find solutions of the most diverse types. There are, however, a handful of approaches that could be considered common to the latest preferences in contemporary interior design: a certain tendency to clear spaces of ornamental objects that obscure and blur architectural lines, the almost systematic elimination of the habitual resources used to disguise load-bearing structures, a trend toward transparent spaces with few spatial divisions, and the recurring use of light and color as integral components of the architectural solutions. In summary, this book presents a selection of the most interesting proposals in interior design, showing a return to more humanized concepts based on the profound relationship of humankind with its inhabited space.

SIMONE MICHELI

Bussotti Residence

Venturina, Livorno, Italy   *Photographs: Mario Corsini*

The Bussotti House is a work of global architectural, an expressive space in which furniture and surfaces only partly reveal their given primary function, transcending their traditional role to relate in original new ways. The visitor discovers a pseudo-museum-like space, an installation of the architecturally unexpected, in which furniture becomes an art that is both surprising and moving. The main feature of the spectacular entrance space is the wide hall, with a floor of oak planks, out of which the elegant kitchen area emerges: this consists of a sculpture and an island, both painted white, with a stainless steel range, illuminated from above by white ceramic floodlights. The non-kitchen conceals the accessories and avoids its stereotyped role as container. The cupboards are equipped with push-open mechanisms. On the entrance wall, a large liquid crystal TV screen violates the ethereal grace of the creased white textile wall covering. The oak stairway rises sculpturally; the railing describes a spiral that starts close to the ground but reaches a height of six feet when it gets to the top; its thickness also varies on the way up. The first floor parapet is a sheet of Visarm tempered glass, illuminated by a line of spotlights in the floor.

From the first floor landing you see the main room, featuring an oak floor and a pillar and beam painted bright green. The materials are used with care and the few incisive signs are manifested in the furniture, with pure and essential lines: a hidden cupboard is virtually second white painted wall, with different sized apertures. The push-open system used throughout avoids the traditionally omnipresent knobs. From one of these apertures, a nondoor lees to one of the upstairs bathrooms, where the white epoxy resin walls set off the glass and steel wash basin. To the left of the stairs, another white painted wall also conceals more cupboard space; one of the openings leads to the elegant main bathroom, divided in three parts with refined but bold wall coverings that separate the areas: in the shower, travertine marble shows off the chromed taps and white sanitary equipment, corium frames the center and the wash basin area, and mirrors surround the dressing area.

The main bedroom is equipped with a large steel based bed, in front of which is a wardrobe completely faced with mirrors. In it is a liquid crystal TV set of which only the screen can be seen; the bed head wall is upholstered in a soft semitransparent curtain material, white and creased, to match the bed cover.

The rooms for the children are amusingly ironic, both functional and refined; no detail has been overlooked. The walls of Niccolò's room are decorated in a zebra pattern of epoxy resin, and the central theme is the stainless steel bed, and the white painted desk. Camilla's room has a bright floor of pale green resin that contains silver CD's.

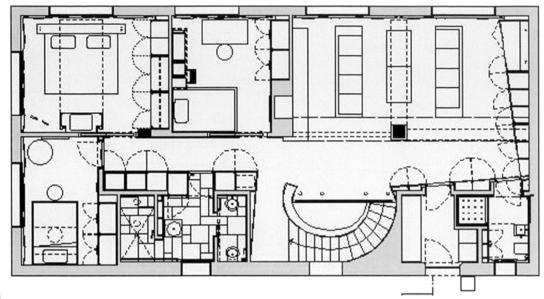

Upper floor plan

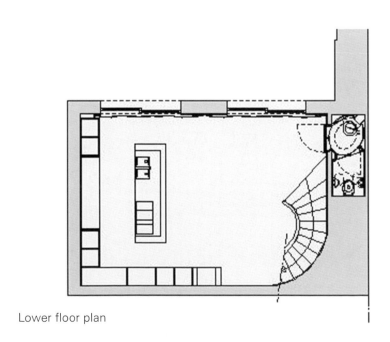

Lower floor plan

Defining the little bathroom is its ellipse shaped first area, which contains the cylindrical corium basin, and a second area in which the wall covering suggests blue bubbles underwater. The water closet is surrounded by two semispherical pieces of furniture enameled in white.

GAP ARCHITETTI ASSOCIATI

Apartment in Via Cicerone

Rome, Italy

Photographs: Filippo Vinardi

The first step in the design process was an unusual brainstorming session, requested by the clients, a young couple with two children. After a tiring yet fun Sunday spent in front of a blackboard and a bottle of white wine, the key concepts for the design were defined: transparency, materialization, flexibility, etc.

The project called for the renovation of an apartment on the second floor of a courtyard building built in the last century in load-bearing masonry. The apartment was divided into two units, which were to be reconnected, with a total floor area of 1399 sq ft (130 sq m). The state of conservation was rather precarious: the paving was damaged and layered; the windows and doors were in a poor state; the wall finishing in some of the rooms was of low quality and full of cracks; the systems were all concentrated in one wet zone. Another interesting feature is the height of the interior spaces at an unusual 13.06 feet (3.98 m).

The clients wanted a large living room and kitchen, a series of work-study areas, the main bedroom, bedrooms for the two children, a space for a live-in nanny, the services, including a small bathroom for guests, and a laundry room.

Given the basic premises, the project found its inspiration in demolishing as much as possible of the existing: in other words, the removal of any non load-bearing elements (in this regard a floor slab dropped some centimeters after the removal of a light partition wall on which it rested, creating immediate problems with the building's residents).

The resulting space became a functional block that defines the use of spaces that were otherwise undefined. This block thickens the central wall and generates a plan that is organized in strips: from the interior they include a hallway, the spine wall, the functional zone and, finally, the apartment proper.

All paving, with the exclusion of the service area, is in saw-cut slate in a running pattern of parallel strips, laid orthogonally with respect to the main organization of the strips in plan. The walls are finished in white stucco; a few walls have been clad in sliding, light diffusing backlit glass panels (the hallway); the main volume features a glass block wall that illuminates the wardrobes behind it.

The significant use of glass allows for a dematerialization of those walls that could not otherwise be eliminated, often in the corridor onto which the narrow entry faces. The metal pieces are painted in anthracite colored ferro-micaceous paint. The wood elements are in waxed, bleached maple.

Due to the previously unexpected fact that the entire building suffers from problems of settlement, which have caused the facade to rotate towards the exterior, with a tendency for detachment from the main building volume, it was necessary to carry out consolidation work using resins to fill the fissures beneath the stucco finish.

The existing shell was entirely stripped of all non load-bearing elements. The metal parts of the new organizational unit that was subsequently designed and installed are painted in anthracite colored ferro-micaceous paint. The wood elements, in contrast, are in bleached and waxed maple.

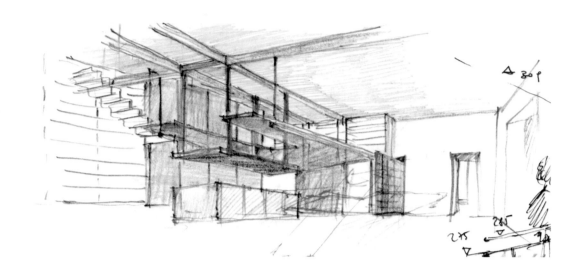

Original building

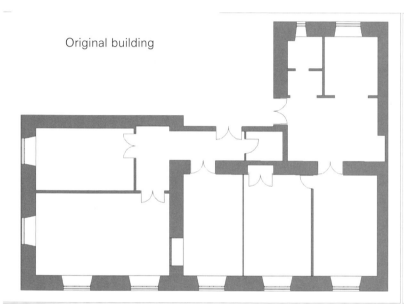

Complete demolition

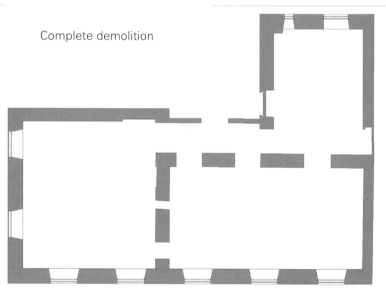

Scheme of functions

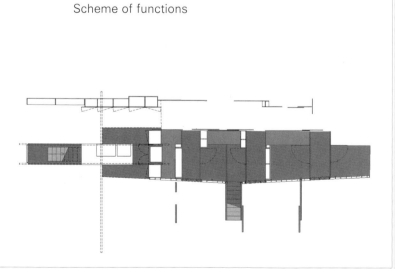

Project

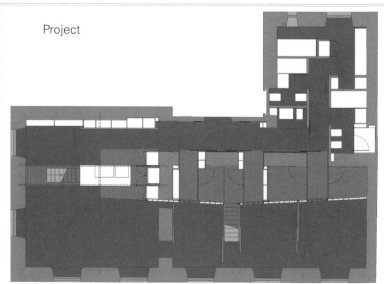

Entrance floor plan

1. Entrance
2. Folding stair
3. Kitchen
4. Living room - dining room
5. Dressing room
6. Parent's bed
7. Children's room
8. Bathroom
9. Guest bathroom
10. Washer - service area

Upper floor plan

1. Folding stair
2. Studio
3. Children's bed
4. Children's closet
5. Private study area

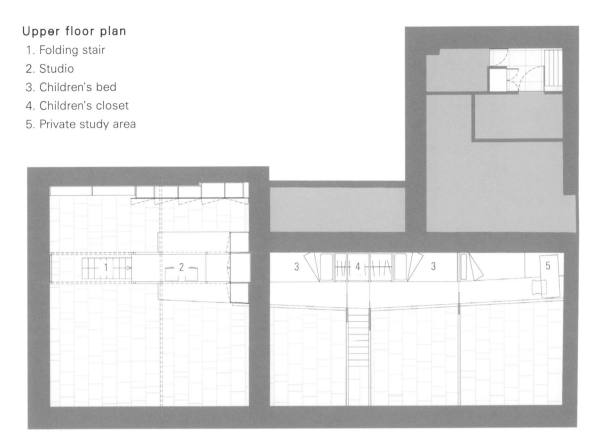

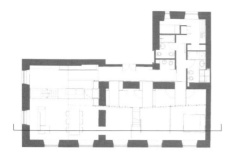

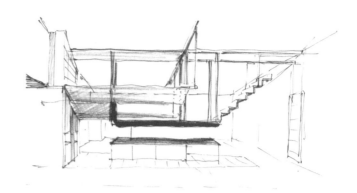

Longitudinal section

1. Folding stair
2. Kitchen
3. Studio
4. Children's room
5. Children's bed
6. Parent's bed
7. Private study area

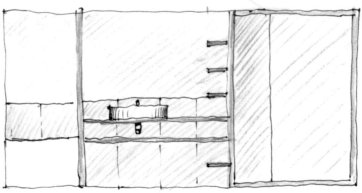

The unusually high ceilings (13 ft or nearly 4 m) enabled a great deal of freedom for inserting new structures and divisions. Almost all of the paving has been done in saw-cut slate set in a running pattern of parallel strips, laid orthogonally with respect to the main organization of the strips in plan.

WHITE DESIGN

Optibo

Göteborg, Sweden

Photographs: Bert Leandersson + Richard Lindor

Traditional living patterns are changing. Today 80% of Göteborg's population lives in one or two person households. Agenda 21, the sustainable development program adopted at the UN conference in Rio de Janeiro in 1992, calls for a 50% reduction of the environmental impact of building by the year 2021. In answer, the Optibo prototype explores the technical, environmental and human possibilities for future living and housing, by incorporating the functions of a 75 sqm apartment into 25 sqm without loss of living quality. The project is a joint venture by different business areas in property, technology, product and building sectors. Optibo is not compact living; it is plenty of room in a limited space: a large room with multiple usage options, instead of many small specialized subdivisions. At the control panel in the hall you can select a number of pre-programmed furniture layouts: much of the furniture has been multi-functionally designed and incorporated into the floor, under which there is a 60 cm space from which chairs, sofas, beds or tables emerge hydraulically to meet different demands. The table's height is variable, from dining to coffee to work station. In the various usage options the character of the flat can be altered by the lighting, for which fiber optics and LED lights have been chosen, with a lifetime of up to 20 years. The apartment's functions are regulated by computer technology. Heating and cooling are delivered automatically through newly developed gypsum panels in the ceiling, the venetian blinds close when the "bedroom" option is activated. At cleaning time, all the furniture disappears and the robotic vacuum cleaner comes out to do the work. The bathroom is accessible through a sliding frosted glass door. The materials and solutions chosen are environmentally sound, tested and used in new ways. Glass is used innovatively in walls, ceilings and kitchen design, combining warmth with a sensation of space. White Design believe the trend of socializing through cooking is set to continue, so a relatively large area in the flat is given to the well equipped kitchen. Naturally, containers for sorting at source are provided. The apartment is easy and cheap to maintain, and represents a contribution to environmental concerns and futuristic housing.

1. Dining room
2. Bath
3. WC
4. Hall
5. Kitchen

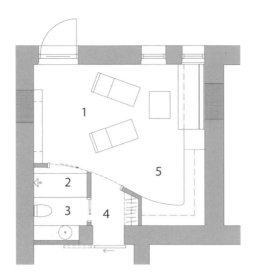

1. Living room
2. Bath
3. WC
4. Hall

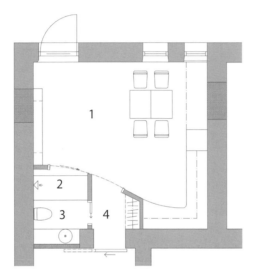

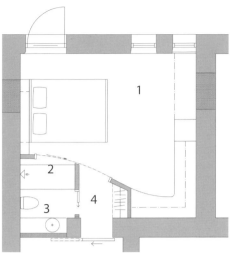

1. Workroom
2. Bath
3. WC
4. Hall

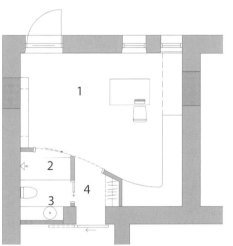

1. Bedroom
2. Bath
3. WC
4. Hall

JYRKI TASA

Moby Dick House

Espoo, Finland

Photographs: Jyrki Tasa, Jussi Tianen

This biomorphic house designed for a family of four is perched on a base of massive natural rocks. A stairway built from stone and a steel bridge lead to the main entrance on the first floor above ground level. One enters the building, which has a surface area of approximately 6135 sq ft (570 sq m) through an organically-shaped, stark white outer wall. On this floor there is a living-room (with a steel fireplace clad in brushed aluminum plates), a library, master bedroom and two balconies. The ground floor houses the children's spaces, a guestroom and a garage. The basement contains sauna facilities, a fireplace and a gym.

The various spaces are alternately connected via three translucent bridges made of glass and steel. Changes in level are joined by an impressive double-height winter garden and a tall spiraling staircase, which features a steel shell with oak steps and a tubular steel handrail with steel wires. This staircase, which forms the spatial core of the house, is lit by a large skylight. From the staircase one has a view in all directions of the house - either directly or through diverse glass walls.

The organically-shaped ceiling on the first floor complements the free-form spatial organization suggested by the curved white outer wall. All interior walls are rectangular in section, as opposed to the outer shell, which forms a dynamic contrast between the two. Large windows expose the house to views toward the southwest and the garden in order to capture the best light in the winter. The house's energy system is complemented by underfloor heating.

The structural framework of the house consists of concrete-filled steel pillars and composite slabs of concrete and steel combined with a roof construction in steel and wood. The facades are mostly clad in plywood, along with pine slats and boards. The undulating first-floor ceiling consists of overlapping birch veneer plates, making it possible to cover the organic form bending in two directions.

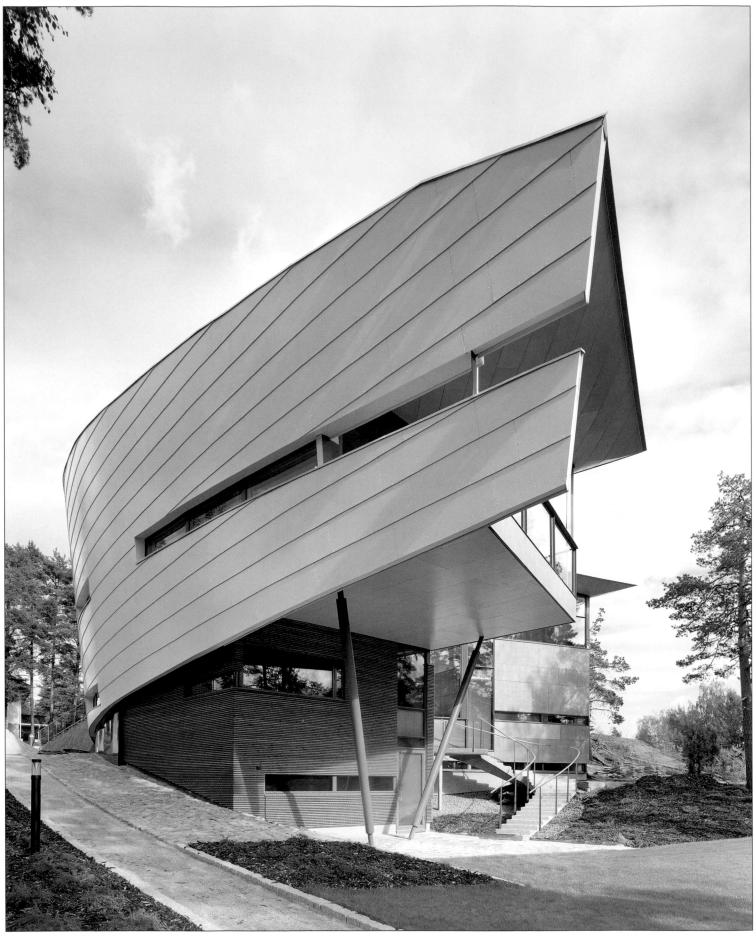

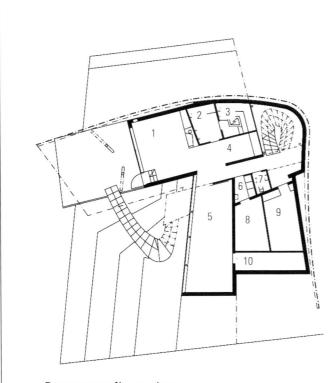

Basement floor plan

1. Sauna cabinet
2. Bathroom
3. Sauna
4. Dressing room
5. Gym
6. Cleaning room
7. Toilet
8. Technical equipment
9. Wine cellar
10. Storage
11. Bedroom
12. Clothes store
13. Bedroom
14. Winter garden
15. Hall
16. Garage
17. Terrace
18. Study
19. Living room
20. Clothes
21. Kitchen
22. Utility room
23. Balcony

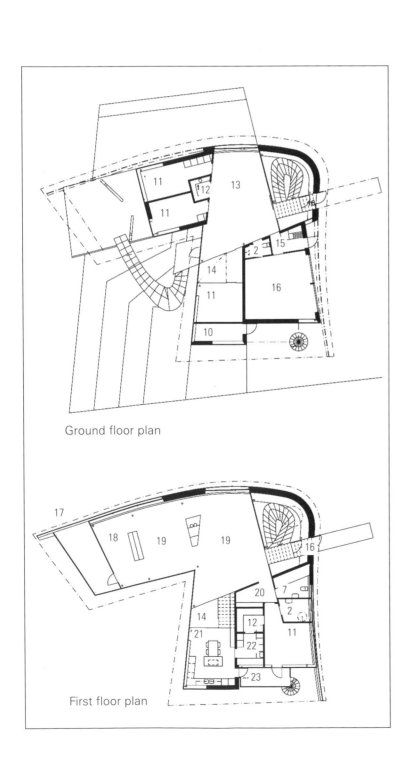

Ground floor plan

First floor plan

53

ATELIER TEKUTO

Cell Brick House

Tokyo, Japan

Photographs: Makoto Yoshida

Cell Brick House sits on the corner lot of a tranquil Tokyo residential area. Tokyo based architect Yasuhiro Yamashita constructed the building, and the skin layering helps create a unique dwelling that applies a new form of masonry. He calls this form of construction "void masonry". The boxes do not serve just to make structure, but also become storage units in the house's interior. They also work to create a brise-soleil light control, allowing the building to respond to the heat of the environment.

The steel boxes used here measure 900 x 450 x 300 mm, and the thickness of the portion facing outside stands at 9 mm. By piling them up in units rather than individually they succeeded in creating a modern design. Since the assembled box units do not fit together perfectly, light is brought into the interior at periodic intervals.

Among the several novel ideas that the client proposed for the project, one example is the bathroom, which is situated so as to appear to be floating; another such idea incorporated into the design was the washing machine sitting on the way up a spiral staircase.

The building takes up three levels from the first floor basement area encompasses 32.93 sqm with a total built area of 85.05 m2, and a height of 6.685 meters. In the next project, they constructed the structure of glass blocks, semi-translucent blocks and transparent blocks, instead of steel boxes.

At first glance, the Cell Brick House seems to be a structure of piled-up concrete blocks, but on closer inspection one sees that these blocks are in fact steel boxes.

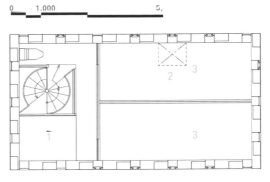

Third Floor   2. Top light

1. Loft   3. Bedroom

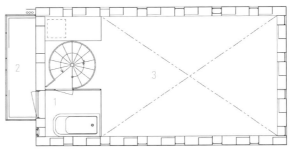

Second Floor   2. Terrace

1. Bathroom   3. Void

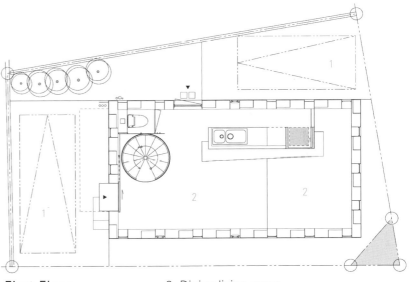

First Floor   2. Dining-living room

1. Car   3. Bedroom

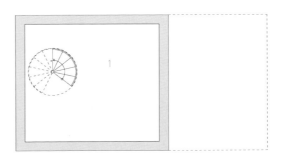

Ground Floor   1. Room 1

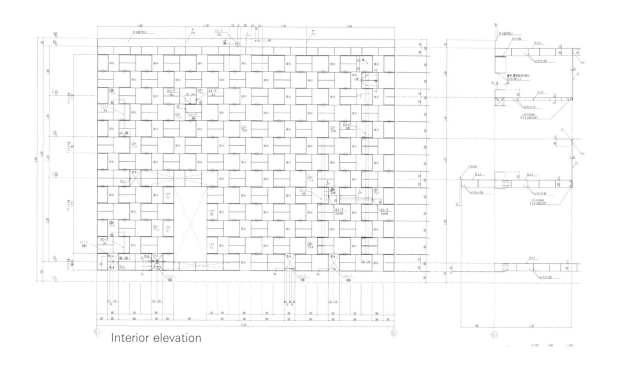

Interior elevation

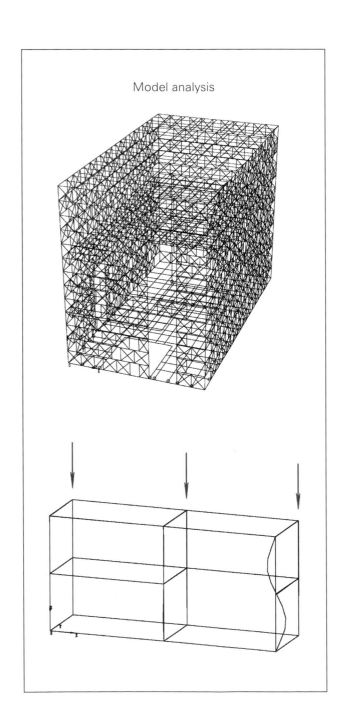

Model analysis

The house is for a family of three: a single parent and two children. The facade's composition of alternating steel blocks and voids is seen in the interior as a succession of storage spaces broken up by dozens of windows that bring abundant natural light into the home.

STRINDBERG ARKITEKTER AB

Villa Näckros

Kalmar, Sweden

Photographs: James Silverman

Situated on the east coast of Sweden, Villa Näckros is a world away from the traditional 'houseboats' of the past. Where floating homes have always been restricted in terms of both space and comfort, this one offers a spacious, contemporary living environment that combines all the luxuries of the modern day home with the spatial freedom and unrivalled views that only waterfront living can provide. One of Strindberg's key design solutions was to use repetition where possible. This worked to both simplify the construction process and help keep costs down. A spacious, light-filled home was achieved, in part, by dividing the space into a number of split-levels.

Encompassing 1916 square feet (178 square meters) of living space, set over three half levels, as well as a roof garden and terrace, the Villa's square shape evolved from the need to create a structure that would be as stable as possible. "We had to create something that would float, but designing a portable home was not the main objective in this case," explains Strindberg. "There was no need to assume the traditional shape of a boat."

The hull is constructed from reinforced concrete, which has been externally isolated to eliminate moisture on the inside. The weight of the concrete, combined with the shape of the hull, provides optimum stability. This method of construction has now been patented by the company. "Everything is glued together; there are no mechanical fastenings."

The main living area is characterized by large floor-to-ceiling windows, again overlooking the water. Oak flooring and neutral walls provide a blank canvas upon which to showcase the room's almost sculptural furnishings. Swathes of light also enable innovative pieces, such as the large white sculpture by Swedish sculptor Eva Hild and Olga Thorson's handmade ceramic 'Woman' lamp to create their own playful shadows across the floor. In the corner, a fireplace draws the eye upwards, emphasizing the room's double ceiling height. Carpeting has been used to subtly sub-divide and define the open plan living space, while Mats Theselius's Ambassad chairs, with their coppered steel frames upholstered in rivet prime leather, provide the perfect accompaniment to Mats Lindehoff's Kub tables.

Downstairs, the bedrooms have been designed with simplicity in mind. Built-in wardrobes create a clean line around the room's perimeter while the blind provides privacy without restricting the room's primary light source. A second of Olga Thorson's limited edition ceramic lamps - this time, 'Man' - provides an element of continuity whilst retaining its unique individuality.

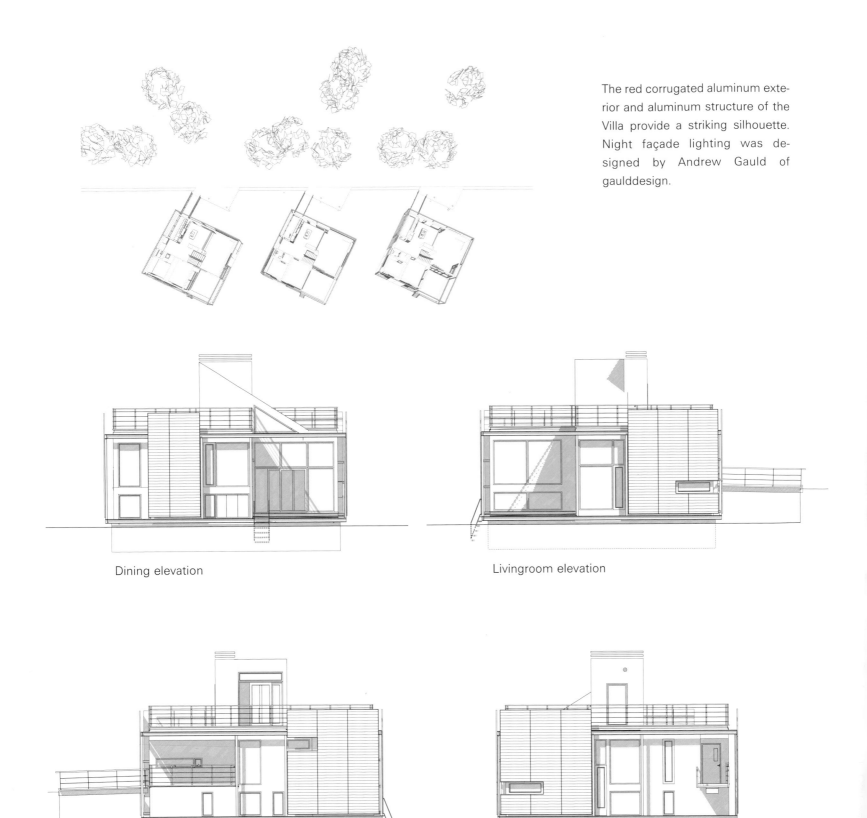

The red corrugated aluminum exterior and aluminum structure of the Villa provide a striking silhouette. Night façade lighting was designed by Andrew Gauld of gaulddesign.

Dining elevation

Livingroom elevation

Entrance elevation

Kitchen elevation

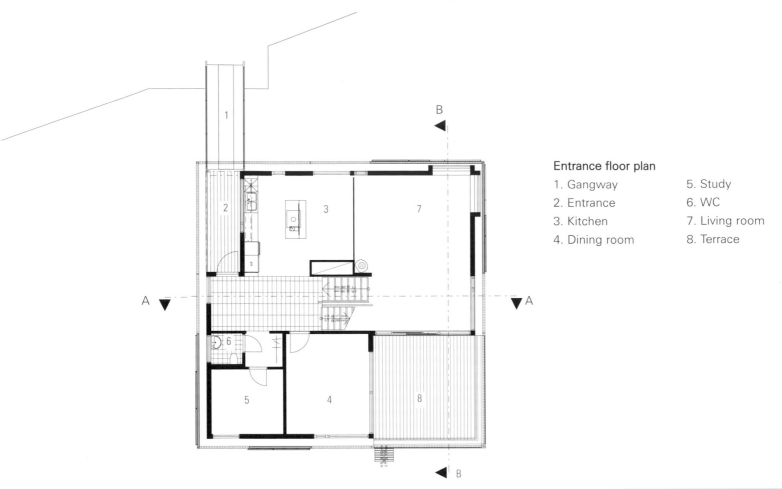

Entrance floor plan

1. Gangway
2. Entrance
3. Kitchen
4. Dining room
5. Study
6. WC
7. Living room
8. Terrace

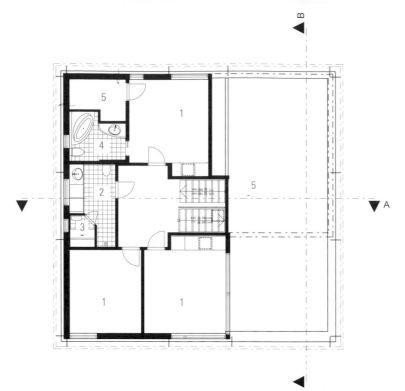

Ground floor plan

1. Bedroom
2. Bathroom / Laundry
3. Sauna
4. Bathroom
5. Mechanical equipment room
6. Store

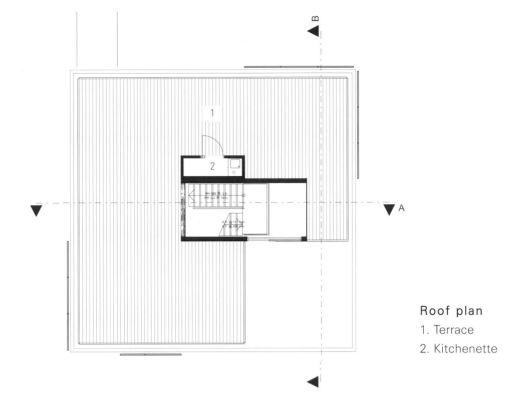

Roof plan
1. Terrace
2. Kitchenette

Section AA

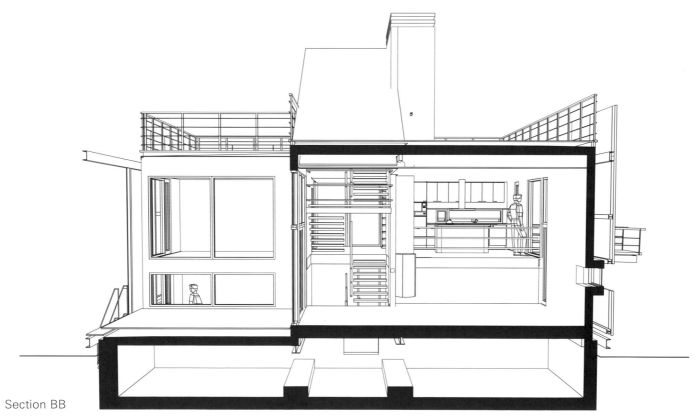

Section BB

BOPBAA

Loft in Barcelona

Barcelona, Spain   *Photographs: Eva Serrats*

This program turned an industrial-sized space (with 39.4 foot (12 m) heigh ceilings) into a habitable leisure zone.

The strength of the project rests on the occupation of the void; here, the stairway visually dominates the space, as well as organizing the route through the various rooms and lofts, from the most social to the most intimate.

The entryway is located on one of the edges of the triangular floor plan. The living room has been positioned so as to capture the best views framed by considerably expansive - both in height and width - picture windows. A couple of steps lead to a new level, thereby separating the entryway from the living room and preparing the dais that culminates at the existing windows, reducing the parapet and creating the overwhelming effect of an open façade.

Slightly shifted onto a side wall, the wooden dais buckles and forms the first flight of the stairway.

This motion enables the unfolding of the dividing wall in order to conceal a small restroom and closet, which itself is the foundation for the second hanging flight of the stairway.

The first loft is the kitchen/dining room. It serves as a roof to the entryway and remains open, balcony-style, to overlook the double-height space of the living room, thus enhancing the relationships with the more public spaces of the loft.

The next flight of stairs leads to the loft-bedroom, which in turn is the roof of the living room. Even midway between levels is a loft-bathroom which opens onto a small terrace at the uppermost point. Visual continuity is also established between these private environments.

The network of lofts is laid out so as to create a large courtyard where the visual relations between the varying levels meet. It is this system of connections, after all, that actually ties the volume together.

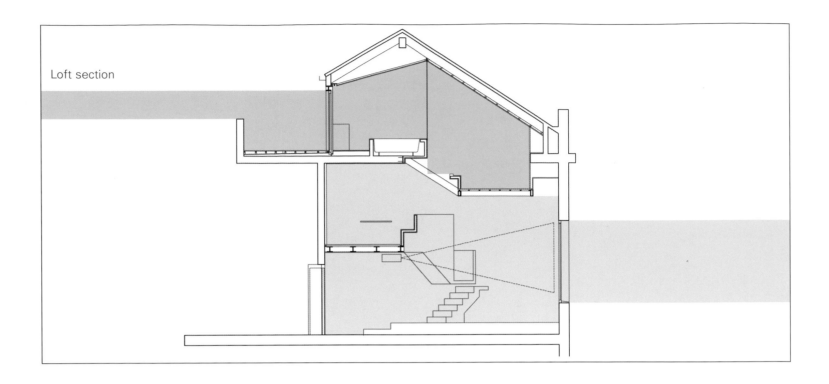

Loft section

The strength of the project rests on the occupation of the void; here, the stairway visually dominates the space, as well as organizing the route through the various rooms and lofts, from the most social to the most intimate.

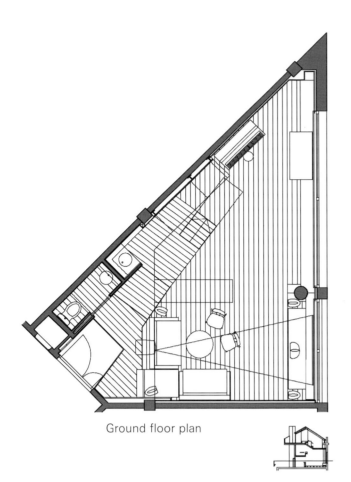

Ground floor plan

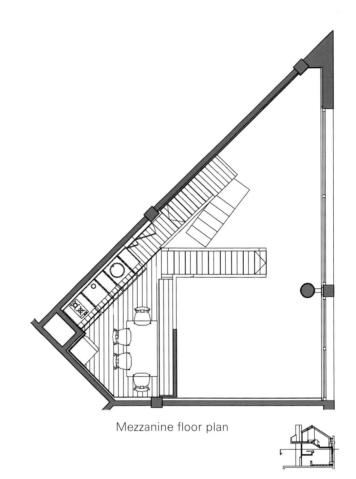

Mezzanine floor plan

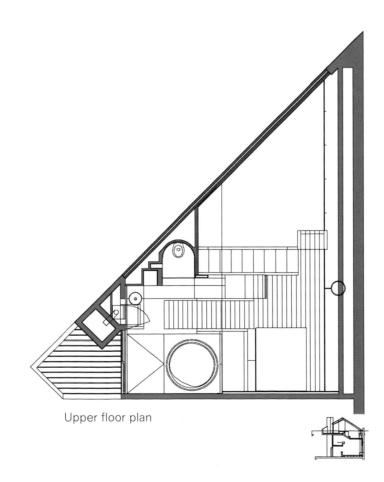

Upper floor plan

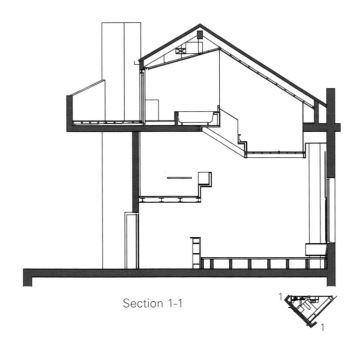

Section 1-1

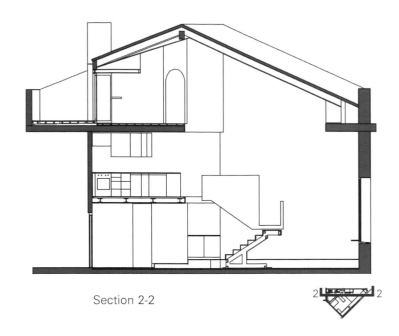

Section 2-2

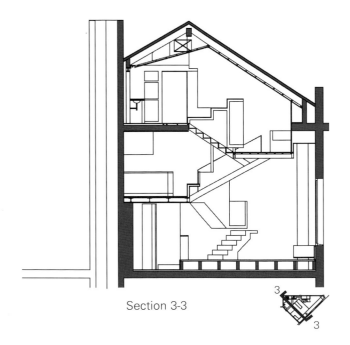

Section 3-3

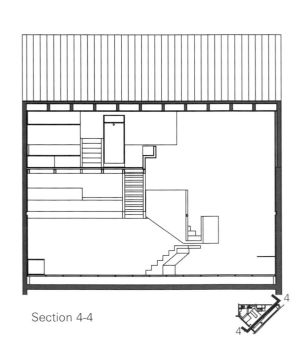

Section 4-4

DAWSON BROWN ARCHITECTURE

James-Robertson House

Mackeral Beach, NSW, Australia

Photographs: Anthony Browell and Patrick Bingham-Hall

Located on a steep, 45 degree, northeast-facing slope on the western foreshores of Pittwater to the north of Sydney, the site is surrounded by the Ku-ring-gai National Park.

The block extends from the rocky shore past a cliff dominated by an ancient fig tree to the boulder-strewn slope just below the ridgeline. The ridges are characterized by large overhanging sandstone caves.

The house is a series of glass, steel and copper pavilions designed to blend into a stunning natural environment. The lower pavilions are grounded on a massive sandstone retaining wall excavated from the site and engineered to geo-technically stabilize the slope. Arrival involves a boat trip, beach walk and slow hill climb to the enclosing rampart walls of the entry.

The sloping walls lead to the first level bamboo grove with its study, guest bedroom and cellar linked by the huge cantilevering floors of the pavilions above.

The path continues up past the copper-clad walls of the main double-height living pavilion to the original cliff face adorned with the hanging roots of a giant fig tree.

It is here that the fully transparent glass pavilions are revealed and the path continues past the louvered and meshed pantry to the central spine adjoining the kitchen /dining room. This in-between space/verandah links the pavilions and main outdoor deck and disappears when the pavilions are fully opened; it is covered by interlocking layers of steel hoods and copper roofs.

The pavilion form with its large overhangs and warped roof planes privatize the glazed spaces from the neighboring constructions, while also drawing in afternoon light and keeping out the summer sun and rain. Through their small-scale, layout, dark colors and materials, the buildings consciously endeavor to diminish their presence as structures in the National Park.

Steel was selected for its resistance to white ants, bushfires and strength; it has been painted black and designed with a minimum section, while the pavilions are nearly invisible in their structural support.

All material/labor access to the site was by boat or barge to a temporary wharf built over the rocks on the shoreline. Steel or heavy items had to be flown in via helicopter due to the handling difficulties.

The openness of the pavilions captures the shore breezes, while the heat of the sun is screened by hoods. Mechanical metal blinds and large overhangs naturally keep the structures cool in the summer. In the winter, warmth is gained through the open fireplace and radiant heating foils in the ceilings.

The home is particularly sensitive to environmental conditions and responds well to a conservationist ethos. Copper was used extensively for roofs and walls to provide a lasting material with a patina, as it will develop beautifully in this marine environment.

The building collects and stores its own water as well as treating its own waste; it relies on catching the breezes to stay cool and consumes minimal energy for heating.

Site location

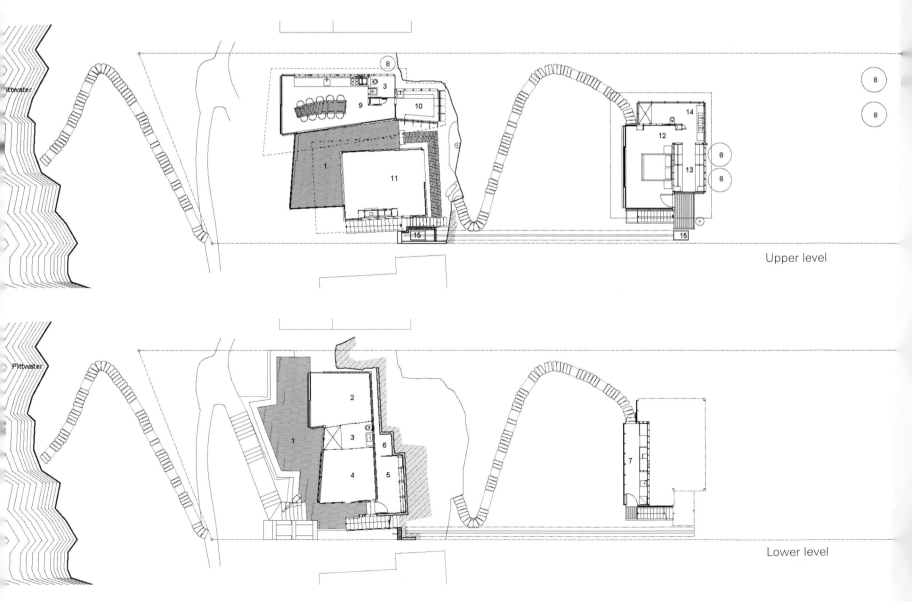

Upper level

Lower level

PROCTER: RIHL

Slice House

Porto Alegre, Brasil

Photographs: Marcelo Nunes, Sue Barr

The Slice House project was selected to represent Brazil in the IV Latin American Architecture Biennale in October 2004 in Peru. The house makes a series of references to modern Brazilian architecture as well as adding a new element with its complex prismatic geometry, which generates a series of spatial illusions in the interior spaces. The project is placed on a site measuring 12.14 feet in width and 126.31 feet in length (3.7 m X 38.5 m). Having been vacant for more than 20 years, it had already gone to auction 3 times without any interest whatsoever. The present client was the only one to put in an offer on the 4th auction, as the general bidders could not see the potential.

The project that was eventually decided upon for the renovation uses prismatic geometry with flush details, which demands more careful detailing and site supervision. Remodeling in 3D allowed adjustments to ensure accuracy and precision of delivered components with final sizing on site. Windows, metalwork, and cabinetwork were assembled to fit on-site. These elements were crafted precisely, in contrast to the intentionally rough concrete surfaces.

Wood-formed cast concrete was preferred since it is a local tradition, and pre-cast concrete or metal formwork is not generally available for this size of a project. The wood formwork was built in situ with a plank pattern emphasizing wood grain, accidental texture pattern, and imperfections. The ceilings were cast at a slope angle of 10 degrees, a familiar technique in the Brazilian building process. The terrace and swimming pool employ an in situ technology of resin and fiberglass coatings applied on site after the concrete cured completely.

Probably the best feature of the house is the crafted metal work. The 22.97-foot-long (7 m) kitchen counter is a continuous steel slab with 6.56-foot (2 m) cantilevered tables floating off of both ends at the dining and courtyard sides. The thick steel plate folds up transitionally between the lower dining height and higher work counter. The steel work surface is coated with avocado-colored, two-part catalyzed laboratory paint providing an extremely hard finish. The stair features a .31 inch (8 mm) steel plate accordion folded and welded in sections onto the undercarriage beam plates. Because the stair is a "U" shape with offset forces, the engineers were able to design thinner and lighter balustrade details than normal.

First floor plan
1. Garden
2. Living room
3. Dining room
4. Kitchen
5. WC
6. Garage utility
7. Garage
8. Bathroom
9. Closet
10. Bedroom
11. Hall
12. Guest room
13. Terrace
14. Pool

NORTH

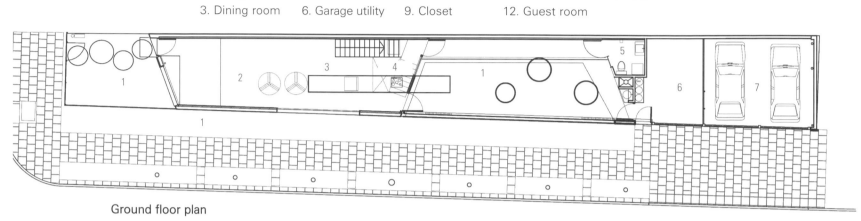

Ground floor plan

© Marcelo Nunes

© Marcelo Nunes

© Marcelo Nunes

105

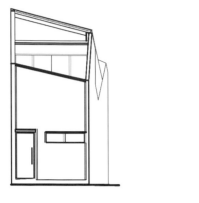

North elelvation

South elelvation

The ceilings were cast at a slope angle of 10 degrees, a familiar technique in the Brazilian building process. The terrace and swimming pool employ an in situ technology of resin and fiberglass coatings applied on site after the concrete cured completely.

© Marcelo Nunes

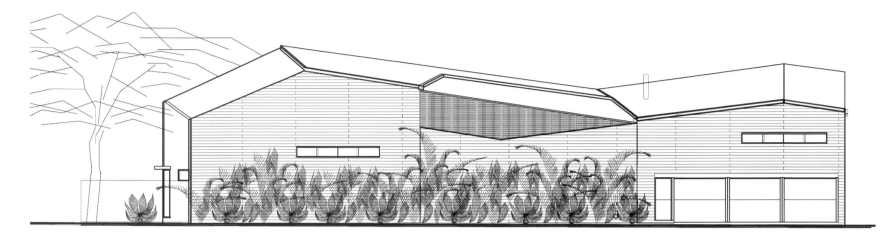

West elelvation

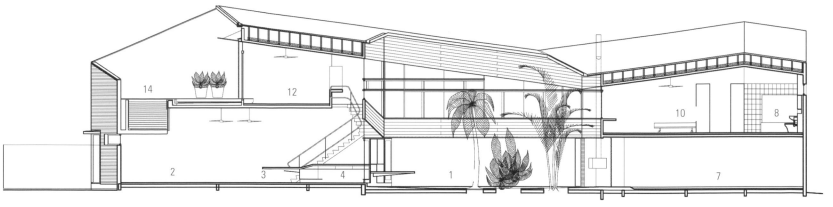

Longitudinal section
1. Garden
2. Living room
3. Dining room
4. Kitchen
5. WC
6. Garage utility
7. Garage
8. Bathroom
9. Closet
10. Bedroom
11. Hall
12. Guest room
13. Terrace
14. Pool

GLEN IRANI

Hover House

Venice, California, USA

Photographs: Undine Pröhl

The Hover House is a live/work prototype designed to resolve typical problems experienced in the contemporary home-office by putting a greater emphasis on the quality of the professional environment. The house envelops 3,500 square feet on three levels, including a studio for the architect, an artist studio for his wife, a residence with guest quarters and outdoor living space, within the confines of a 30 x 90 foot lot along the canals of Venice, California.

The project responds architecturally to the problems facing professionals who work at home through three main strategies. Firstly, by providing opportunities to rest the mind and body during long working hours through amenities such as the garden, terraces and swimming pool. Secondly, it encourages engagement with the community by placing the working area on "prime real estate" - the ground level - with high transparency and accessibility to the public space. Thirdly, it addresses the need for workspace accessibility and privacy by isolating the workspaces from the living areas. The architecture studio is the only habitable space in the garden, so it also readily converts to a living area by sliding the desks to one end on integrated rails.

The massive house that hovers above the ground level program is focused around a large, C-shaped "sun-court" oriented towards the southwest. On the second floor, a children's playroom and the community areas all open onto the sun-court through large sliding glass panels. All the furniture on this level is lightweight and exterior rated so that the courtyard can be furnished quickly and flexibly - as a playground, living area, art studio, dance floor, sunning deck, etc. Children's play areas are all visible from "adult" areas.

The artist's involvement in developing spaces, building systems like windows and objects within them like cabinetry, expresses his interest in manufacturing buildings as opposed to constructing them. Reflecting the preference for manufacturing practices, other than the foundation, framing and wall finishes, much of the house is actually factory fabricated.

Over 40 colors throughout the house, most visible from every area in the house, arose from a fledgling color theory devised by the architect and artist. This theory, while being peripherally concerned with color hue relationships, focuses primarily on the light-reflectance relationships between colors and the vibration of light that occurs when many colors unite in one space. These vibrations articulate movement, mass, time and materiality.

The floor-to-ceiling glass windows flood the interior spaces with light and provide visibility that unifies the house. The colors, the landscaped garden and the swimming pool are part of the strategy to improve the quality of professional and family life by allowing the mind and body to be inspired and rejuvenated.

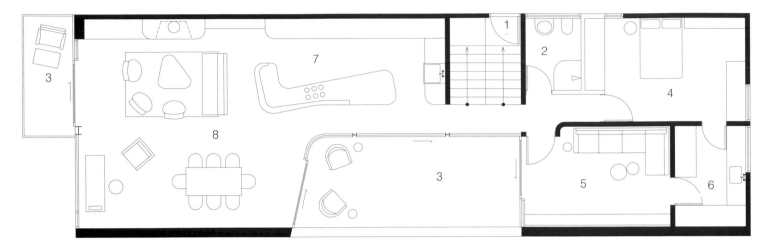

Ground floor plan

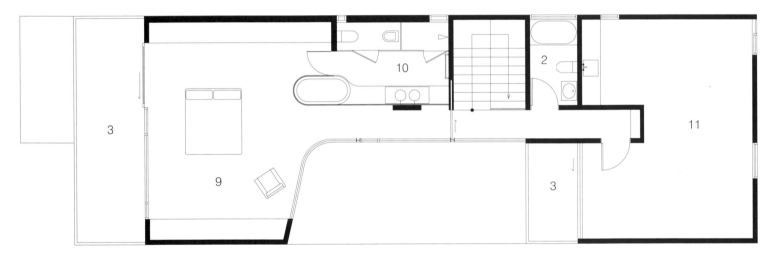

First floor plan

1. Entry	7. Kitchen
2. Bathroom	8. Living / Dining room
3. Outdoor terrace	9. Master bedroom
4. Bedroom	10. Master bathroom
5. Den / Guest bedroom	11. Painting studio
6. Laundry	

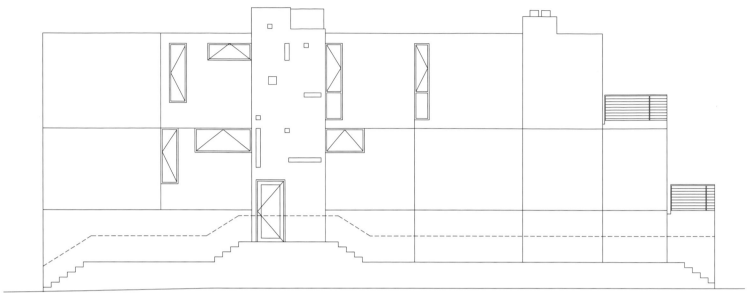

Elevation

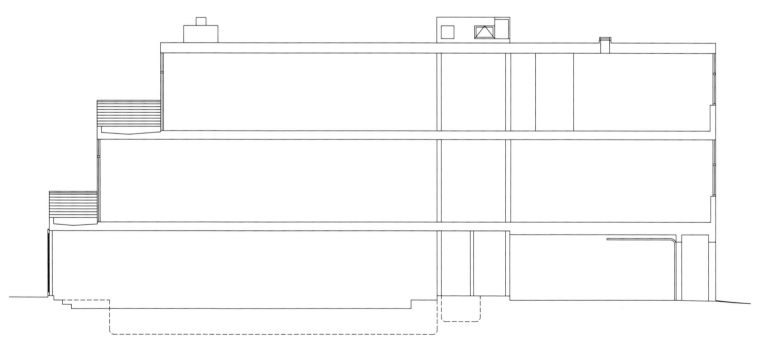

Longitudinal section

Elevation

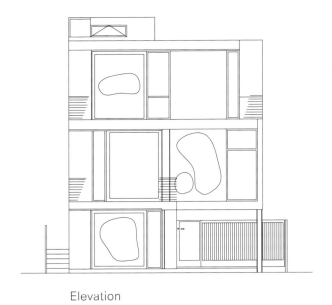

Elevation

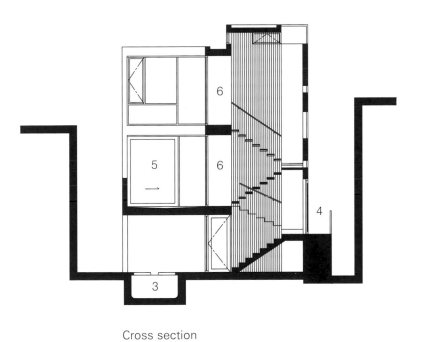

Cross section

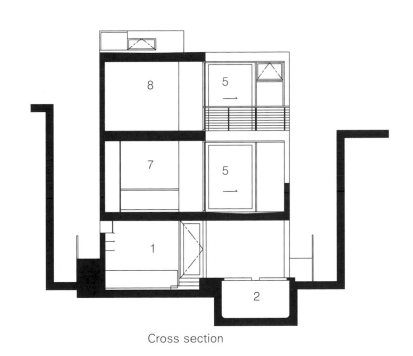

Cross section

Cross section

1. Studio / Office	5. Outdoor terrace
2. Lap pool	6. Hallway
3. Spa	7. Kitchen
4. Entry	8. Master bedroom

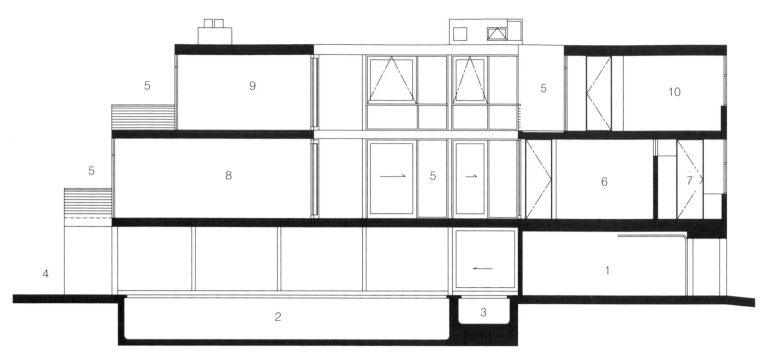

Longitudinal section

1. Garage / Workshop	4. Garden	8. Living / Dining room
2. Lap pool	5. Outdoor terrace	9. Master bedroom
3. Spa	6. Den / Guest bedroom	10. Painting studio
	7. Laundry room	

CHO SLADE ARCHITECTURE

Hochhauser Residence

New York, USA

Photographs: Jordi Miralles

The brief for the renovation of what is now a 2400-square-foot apartment (there were originally two apartments dating from the 1960s, each measuring 1200 sq ft or 111.48 sq m) was as precise as it was varied. The original apartments had to be unified into a single volume for a couple with two daughters, thus necessitating a complete reorganization of the space. The surface finishes (floors, walls and ceilings) were to be stripped and redone. The clients also wanted to maximize on storage space, and at the same time create as much openness as possible without compromising privacy. Finally, the views, particularly those to the south and west, were to be maximized.

These stipulations were met with the architects' solution of creating three zones. The "formal" zone is that housing the living/dining room, an open kitchen, entrance and guest room; the "family" zone encompasses the den, bedrooms and children's bathroom; and, finally, the "master suite" features a study, master bedroom, bathroom and balcony.

Each zone is arranged in a unique spatial configuration generated by the program and the location/orientation of the spaces within the building. The formal zone is a grand space occupying a full third of the whole house with new windows as wide as 14 feet (4.27 m) to capture the spectacular views and natural light of the southwest corner. The family zone is organized along a translucent colored acrylic wall that brings the spaces together with the soft glow of light. The master suite is a pinwheel of volumes arranged along the windows at the northwest corner of the apartment.

Maple flooring and cabinetry tie the zones together, while each space contains its own distinguishing elements. For example, cabinetry in an amalgam of black leather, stone and glass defines the formal zone, while a maple-colored translucent wall frames the family zone, and a dramatic plaster-sculpted Venetian wall/ceiling predominates in the master suite.

These apparently monolithic and monochromatic elements, such as cabinets and built-in furniture, are assembled from different materials with mitered joints to obtain subtle changes in materials at each surface. For example, the black built-in cabinets in the living room have black leather doors, black lacquered sides, black glass at the back and a black stone top. Because the mitered joints conceal the thickness of the materials, the material differences reveal themselves only when you are next to the object - from a distance they appear monolithic.

The "formal" zone of the apartment occupies a full third of the entire apartment and features windows as wide as 14 feet (4.27 meters). The living room is furnished in built-in cabinetry with leather doors, black-lacquered sides, black glass at the back and a black stone top. These apparently disparate materials form a unified whole, due to the mitered joints between surfaces.

EDGE DESIGN INSTITUTE

Suitcase House

Badaling Shuiguan, Beijing, People's Republic of China

Photographs: Howard Chang, Gary Chang

In 2000, SOHO China Ltd. invited 12 young architects from South Korea, Japan, Taiwan, Singapore, Thailand, Mainland China and Hong Kong, to design 11 houses and a clubhouse in the valley at the foot of the Great Wall.

Rethinking the proverbial image of a house, Suitcase House Hotel questions the nature of intimacy, privacy, spontaneity and flexibility, in pursuit of infinite adaptable scenarios, unfolding the mechanics of domestic (p)leisure.

The 2696.356 sqft (250.5 sqm) building, completed in October 2001 at the head of the Nangou Valley, is oriented to maximize views of the Great Wall and solar exposure in the temperate continental climate.

The base of the building's three strata is a concrete plinth, which contains the pantry, a servant's room, the boiler room and the sauna.

The middle layer cantilevers outward from the concrete plinth that anchors the steel structure above. Everything is clad in the same timber, blurring boundaries between in and out, building and furniture. This level is for habitation, activity and flow. The layout is non-hierarchical; movable items of the shell adapt to the activity, number of occupants, or preferences regarding privacy. The open volume turns into a sequence of rooms, each singularized by a specific role. Concealed under a landscape of pneumatically assisted floor panels, several function-specific compartments may be "unfolded". Only what is in use is present at any one time. Besides the basic bedroom, bathroom, kitchen and storage, there is a meditation chamber (with glazed floor looking down the valley), music chamber, library, study, lounge, and a fully equipped sauna. If guests arrive in the evening, the entire space, 144 x161/2ft (44 x 5 m), can turn into a single lounge. If the party goes on late, seven guest rooms can be unfolded, accommodating up to 14 people.

The exterior is an envelope of full height double-glazed folding doors; the inner layer is a series of screens. The façade pattern is rooted in its user-oriented logic. The various entrances hold equal status and their use decides the distribution.

A pull-down ladder leads to the roof, the top stratum, with a 360° view.

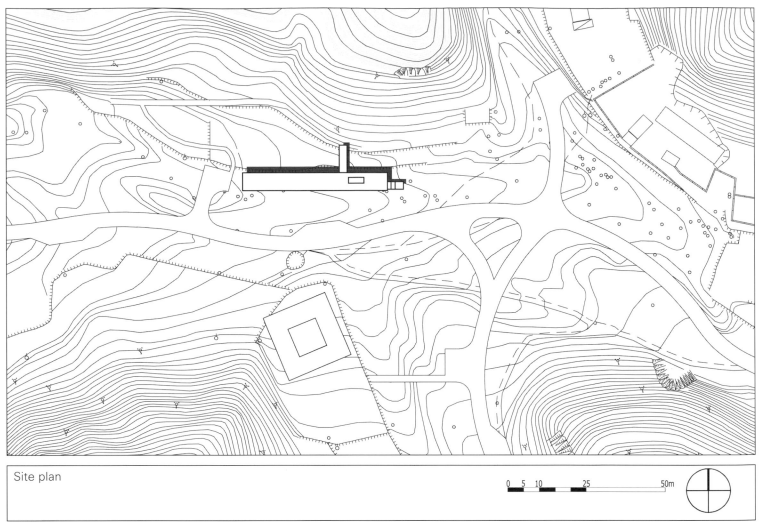

Site plan

0 5 10   25   50m

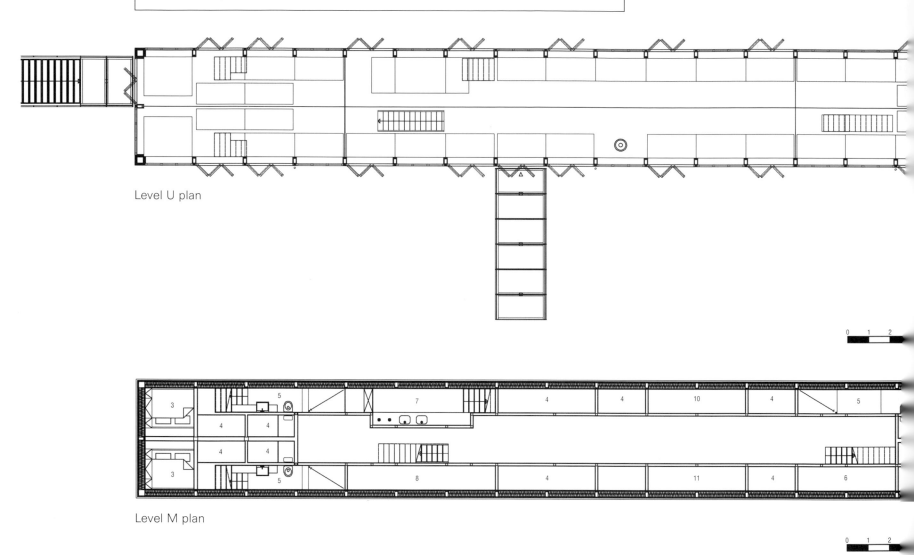

Level U plan

0 1 2

Level M plan

0 1 2

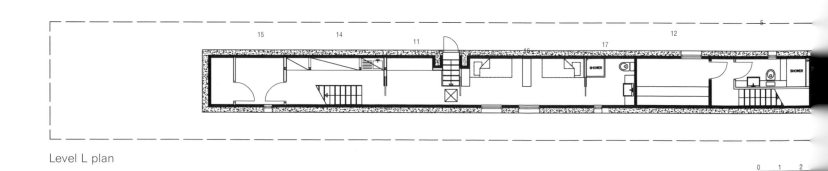

Level L plan

0 1 2

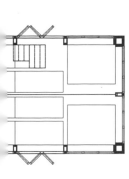

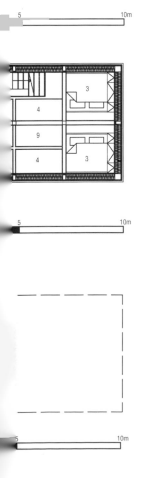

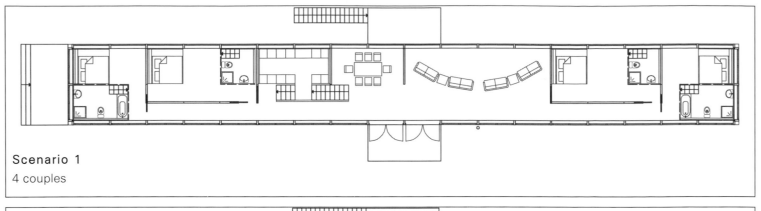

Scenario 1

4 couples

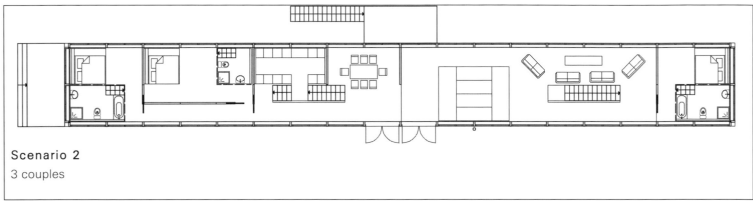

Scenario 2

3 couples

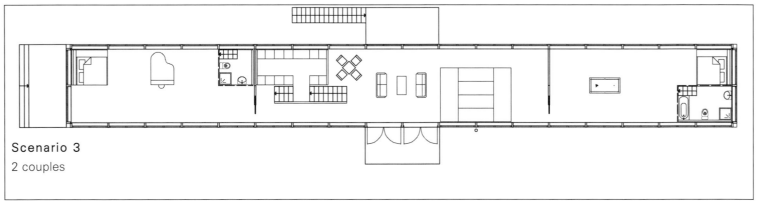

Scenario 3

2 couples

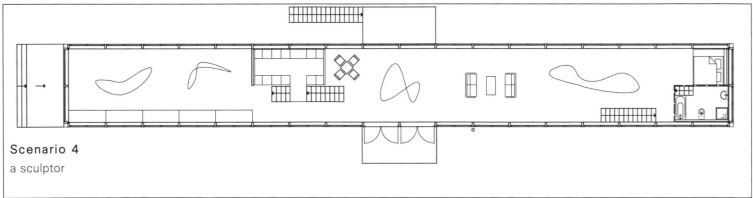

Scenario 4

a sculptor

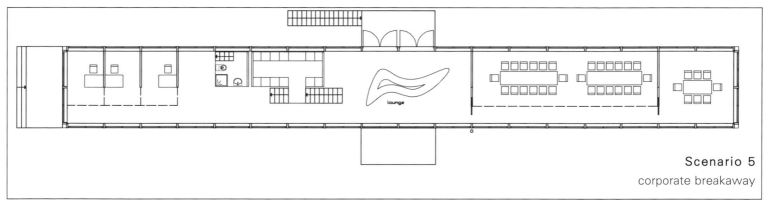

Scenario 5

corporate breakaway

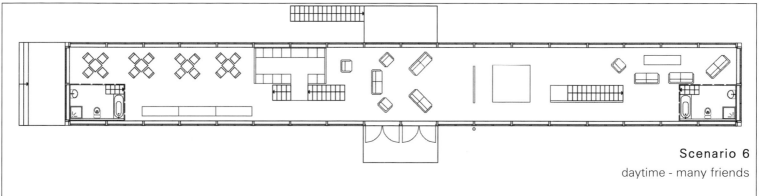

Scenario 6

daytime - many friends

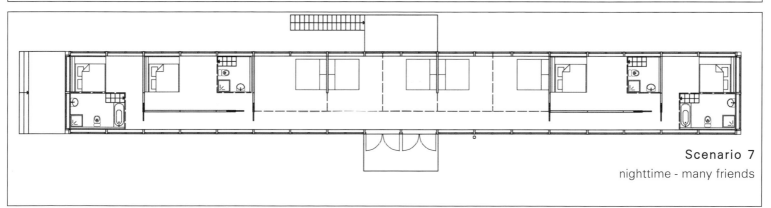

Scenario 7

nighttime - many friends

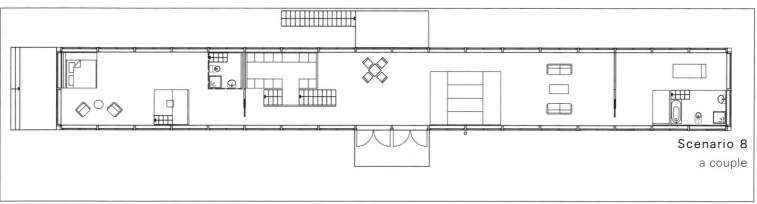

Scenario 8

a couple

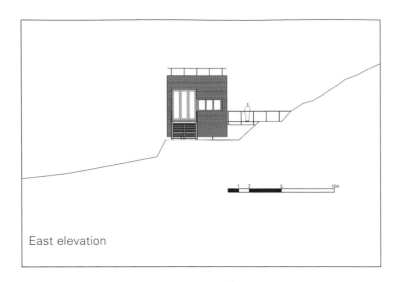

East elevation

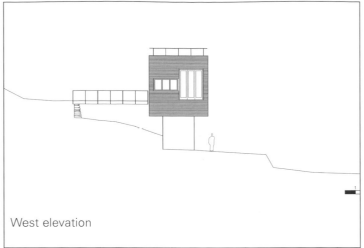

West elevation

South elevation

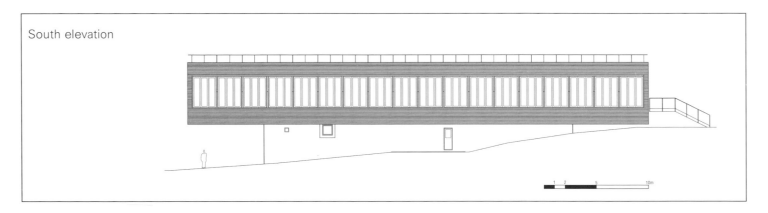

Pneumatically assisted floor panel

1. Location of latch
2. Location of dead-bolt
3. Gas spring
4. Location of hook and eye
   to hold panel in position

5. Recessed hinge
6. Metal bracket
7. Under panel support

Plan

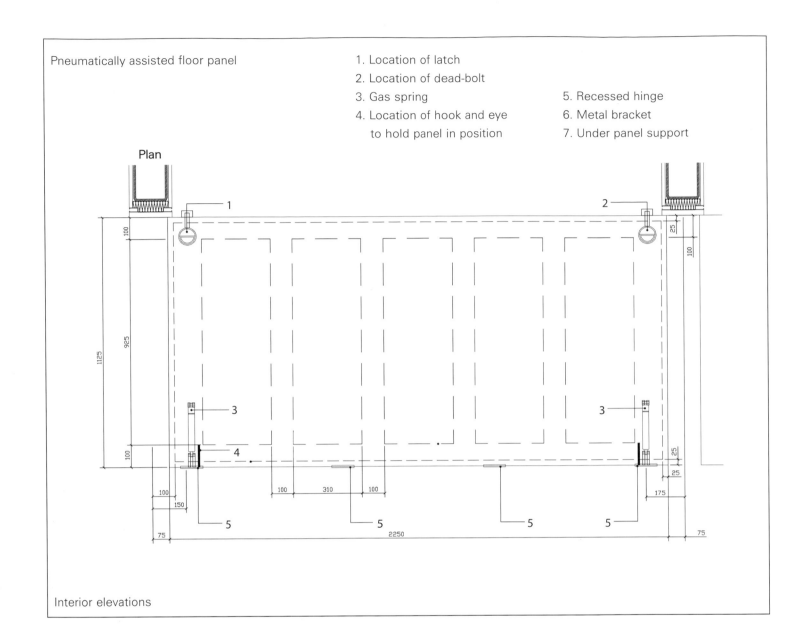

Interior elevations

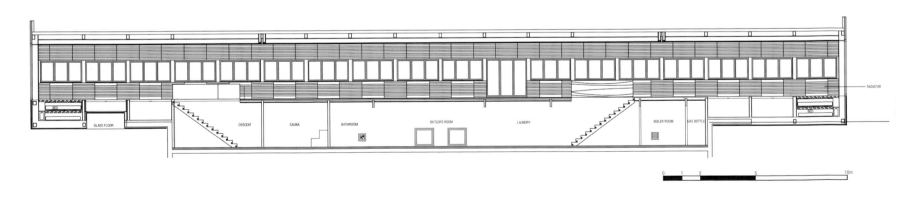

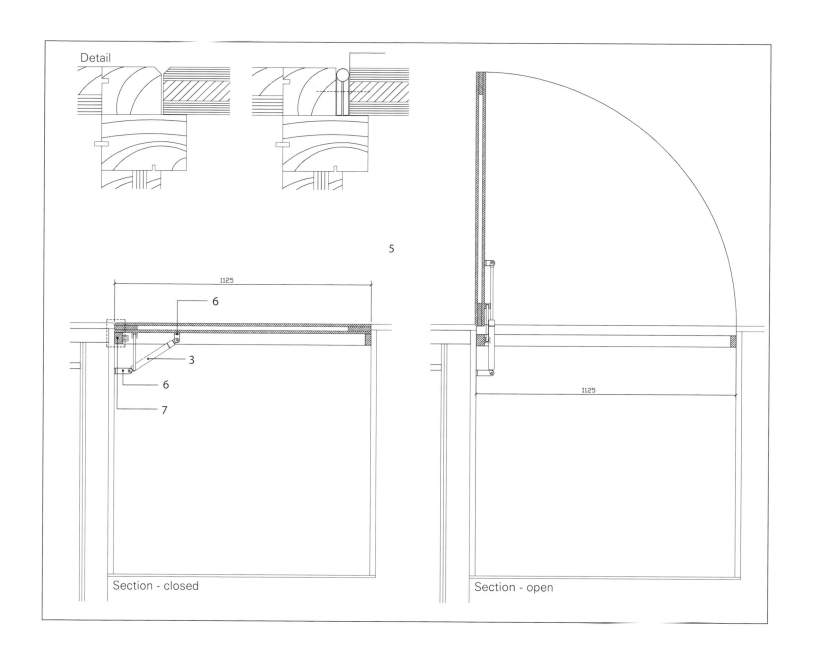

Detail

5

1125

6

3

6

7

Section - closed

1125

Section - open

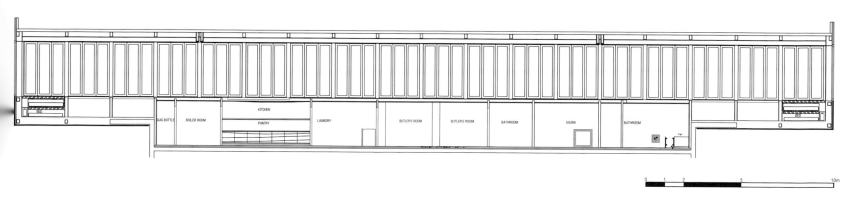

GAS BOTTLE | BOILER ROOM | KITCHEN | LAUNDRY | BUTLER'S ROOM | BUTLER'S ROOM | BATHROOM | SAUNA | BATHROOM

PANTRY

0 1 2 5 10m

Bathroom

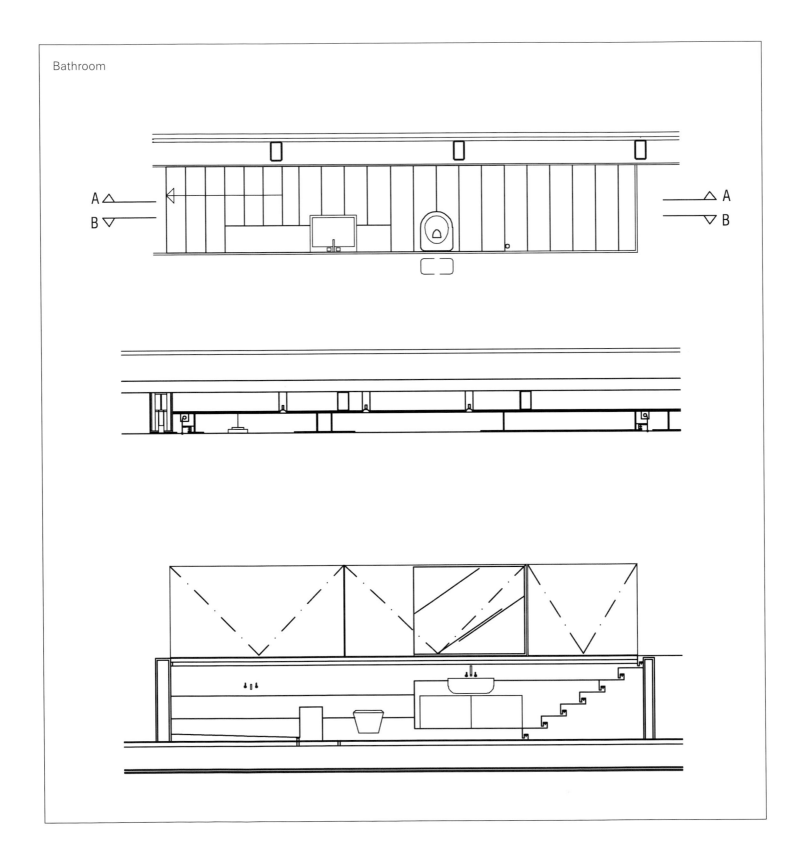

Kitchen

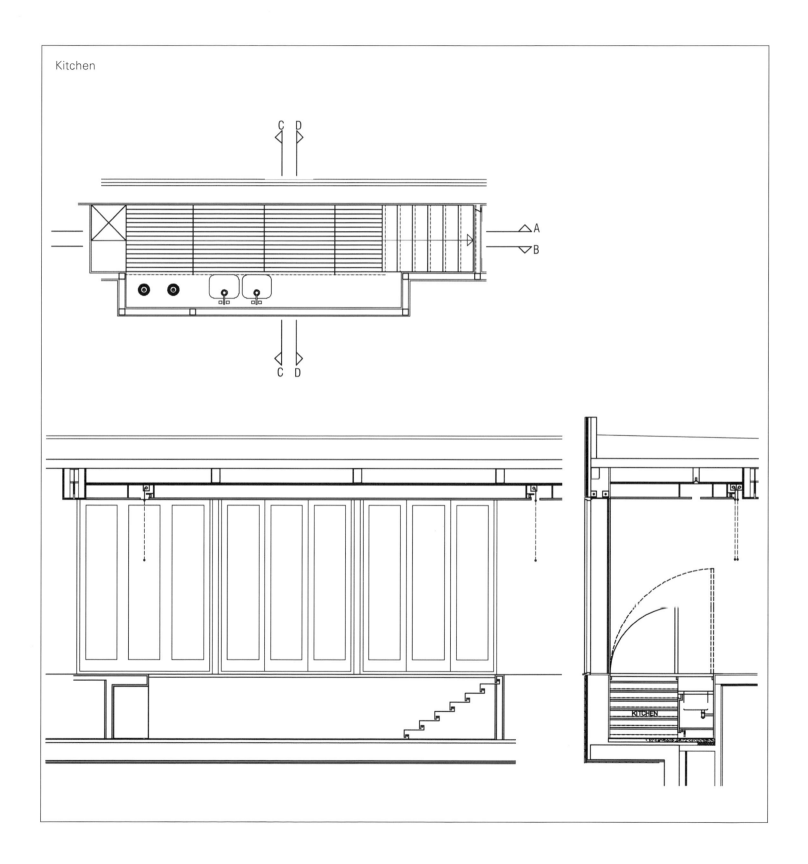

SUGIURA OFFICE

House H

Nagoya, Japan

Photographs: Tamoutsu Kurumada

House H is located in a narrow site surrounded by neighboring buildings. In Japan, this configuration is known as "Unagi no Nedoko" or "the nest of an eel", and it is common in traditional city-house districts in Kyoto, presenting special privacy and space problems for new buildings. This particular site is open to the north, where there is a busy road. The clients wanted to avoid having windows looking out to the road, but they still hoped to have a bright and open house.

Within this narrow site, the architects placed the volume leaving a 2.5 m strip of land to the south and a 1 m strip to the east. These spaces are used to help guide the light and air to the interior in order to create an open feeling inside.

The largest openings were placed on the south side to allow as much direct sunlight as possible into the building. Frosted glass for diffused light was placed on the east-facing side of the first floor. On the western side where there is no setback at all from the neighbors, skylights were designed to allow the light to filter through the roof and floor down to the first floor. At the northern end of the second floor, a kind of chimney acts as a vent to allow air to flow from the south to the north. The resulting space manages to have free flowing air and three different types of light - direct, diffused and changing light - to create a house that feels open.

The structure was designed to take up minimum space. Although it is actually a hybrid that uses both frames and Vierendeel structures, to the observer it appears like a simple box.

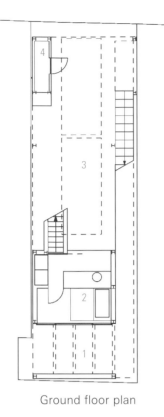

Ground floor plan

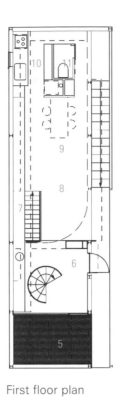

First floor plan

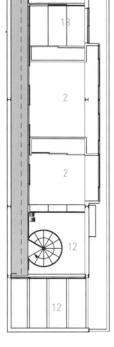

Second floor plan

1. Court
2. Bedroom
3. Parking
4. Storage
5. Terrace
6. Entrance
7. Counter
8. Living
9. Dining
10. Kitchen
11. Lavatory
12. Void
13. Tatami room

153

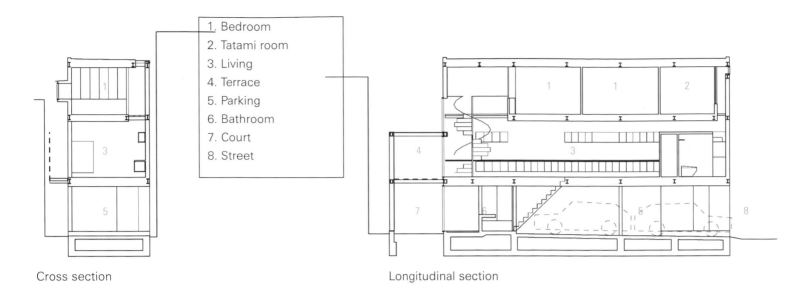

1. Bedroom
2. Tatami room
3. Living
4. Terrace
5. Parking
6. Bathroom
7. Court
8. Street

Cross section

Longitudinal section

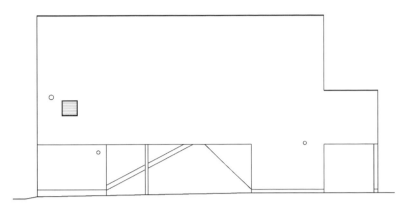

West elevation

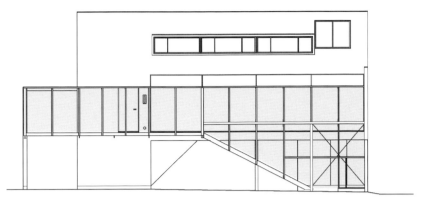

East elevation

The architects use three types of light
- direct, diffused and changing light -
to bring as much light as possible into
the interior while maintaining privacy
from the surrounding buildings.

ROBERTO SILVESTRI

A House in Piazza Navona

Rome, Italy

Photographs: Ernesta Caviola

Designing the interior spaces of a house allows you to work with emotions, to shape rooms that will hold inside feelings, angers, passions, moods. "The house is the life coffer," Le Corbusier used to say. Upon this concept we have based the project for the house of an italian film director; a house that had to gather the private world and the public life of the owner. A house that had to be, at the same time, "coffer" and "theatre" of life.

During the designing process, we have spent a long time together with the client talking about cinema, art, cooking, books, and being careful not to touch on technical problems. The idea was to create an interior space shaped exactly around the client's character and desires, without thinking too much about functional problems that, in this way, would have been naturally solved. For this reason, deep knowledge of the client has been so important; his ideas, his way of moving, his passions and tastes have been the functional program.

Working with these purposes, we managed to make a very sensitive place, a rich but not overwhelming space, a strong but warm and cozy place at the same time. We believe that it is impossible for mankind to live in geometrically perfect spaces, to stay in architecturally pure forms. For this reason, we have designed a rigorous house that speaks with feelings and the imperfections of human life. So the space is extremely open and fluent. The rooms are strictly connected, but at the same time, each single traditional room is still visible in the structure of the house. The house is not loft space, but is a real house divided into rooms that suit the contemporary way of Italian living.

The access to the house comes from above, walking on a three-step stair made of Travertino Navona slabs put on a light iron structure. The living room has very little furniture. The main character of the room is the front wall: dark, brown, velvety, non-homogeneous. This is the first of the two walls that are covered in Cort-ten: rusted iron usually used in exteriors. This material is absolutely perfect for our purposes: it is warm, strong and capable of giving a beautiful atmosphere to the whole room. The two rusted walls form the space of the studio: a small, intimate and high tech place that can easily be transformed into another sleeping room.

The outside terrace is connected to the kitchen that is completely open to the rest of the house. In front of the kitchen, two openings in the ancient wall show the history of the place with its historical bricks made of Roman Tufo. This creates a strange contrast with the modern materials of the new project such as the aluminium wainscoting which is included within the wall itself.

The private spaces are very small: a bedroom and a bathroom. The first one has been designed around the client, so it is a very small place with just a bed and a wardrobe, both made of natural wood. Very different from this is the bathroom; a place for private luxury completely different from the rest of the house. The floor is made of big slabs of red marble that strongly contrast with the white of the walls that are partially covered with a very particular kind of tiles: the same tiles that the client saw in the Paris underground while he was starting an unforgettable love story.

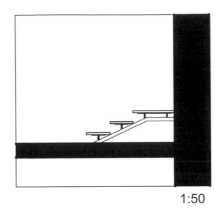

1:50

Plan

A

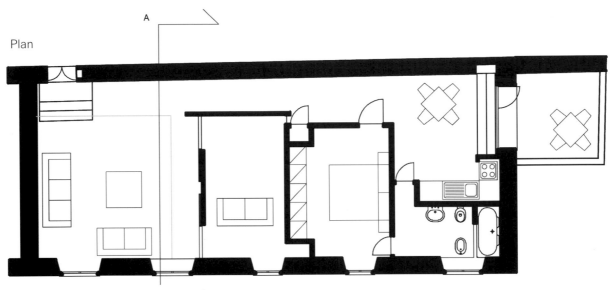

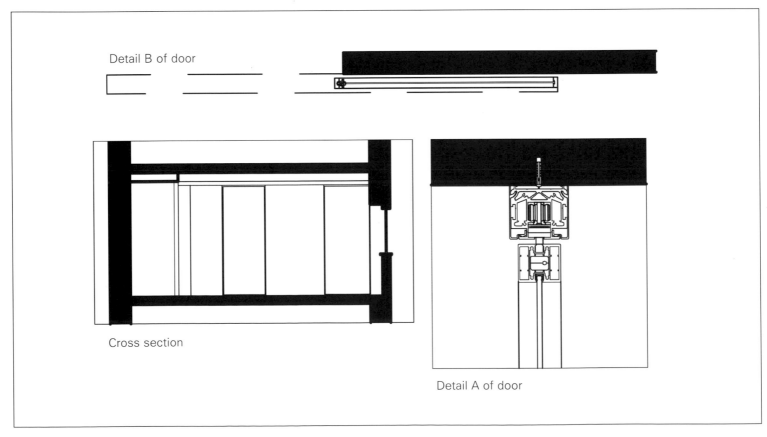

Detail B of door

Cross section

Detail A of door

Wingårdh Arkitektkontor AB

Villa Astrid

Brottkärr, Göteborg, Sweden

Photographs: James Silverman

The dramatic landscape of the Swedish west coast becomes overly domesticated when housing construction takes over. Boulders are terraced to make gardens, wild ravines are transformed into roads and plots of land. The rare places that still have a concentrated atmosphere are those that are left over, being either too difficult to build on or impossible to tame. Villa Astrid has just such a location. The house has not made the setting any less dramatic, instead interpreting the character of the location. The twist away from the road, the steep cliff and the view out towards the sea have been given form using architecture's most fundamental aspects - openness and enclosure. The closed elements, walls and roof, constitute a durable armor of patinated copper plate, while the open elements - the glass sections - appear like carved holes in this solid structure. This sculptural approach could well have stopped at rigid formalism if it weren't for the house's affectionate relationship with nature. Its design has not sprung from principles or abstract theories, but from a summary of the requirements of the site and the provisions for the area for a roof gradient of 14 to 30 degrees and a roof base height of 9.84 feet (3 meters).

The house is closely bound to its site. The rocks on which it stands pose naked inside the house and form a wall in the deep courtyard that brings light to the ground floor living room. The upper-floor rooms, designed for work and leisure, focus on the view, giving the house a counter twist, like a person whose hips and shoulders turn slightly in different directions.

This house has been designed for a middle-aged couple, with one child, who entertain at home a great deal. The contrast between the open character of the entrance floor and the privacy on the ground floor reflects these functions, while the easily hidden dining room, which is also part of the entrance floor, offers a pleasant surprise.

The simplicity of this structure makes it very robust. The concrete joists rest on walls built of lightweight concrete. The tie beam system is insulated with foam glass, sealed with asphalt against the concrete. This provides full insulation under the copper skin. The structure of the house makes it completely waterproof without any incorporated organic materials. Copper ions from the façade can be neutralized by crushed limestone along the plinth.

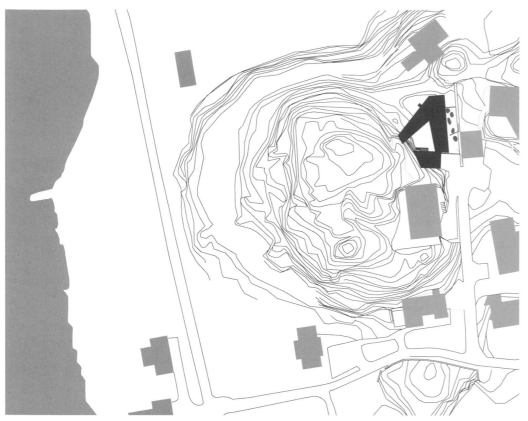

The house is closely bound to its site. The rocks on which it stands pose naked inside the house and form a wall in the deep courtyard that brings light to the ground floor living room.

Site plan

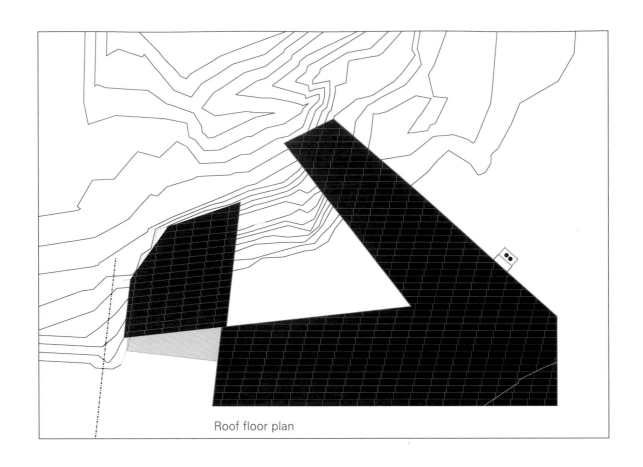

Roof floor plan

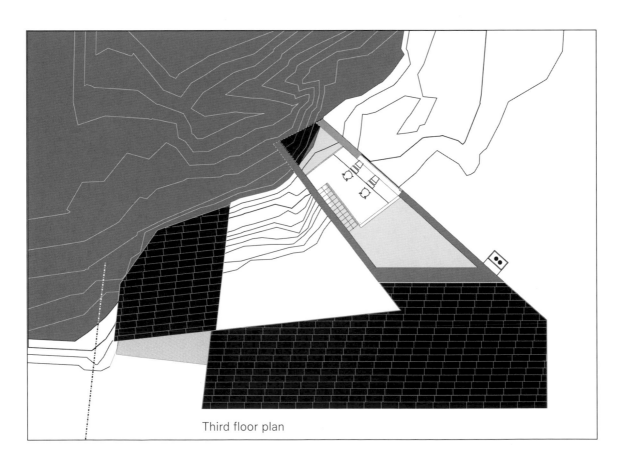

Third floor plan

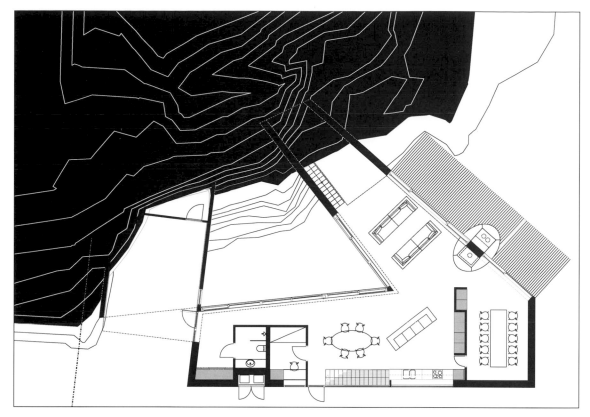

Second floor plan

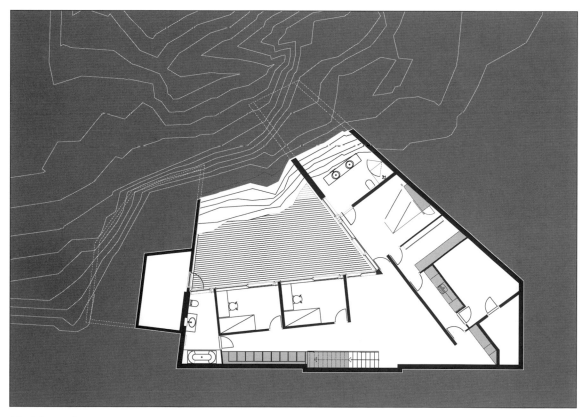

First floor plan

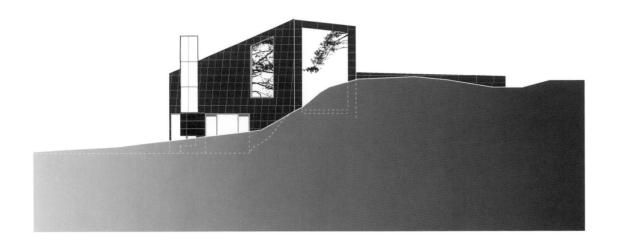

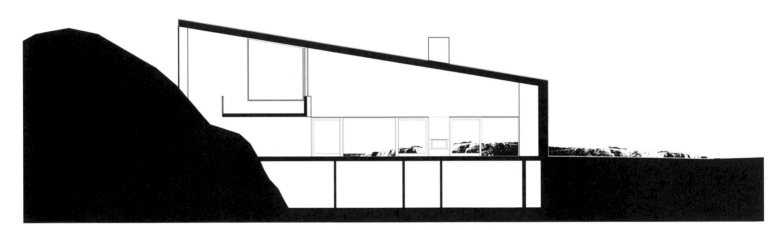

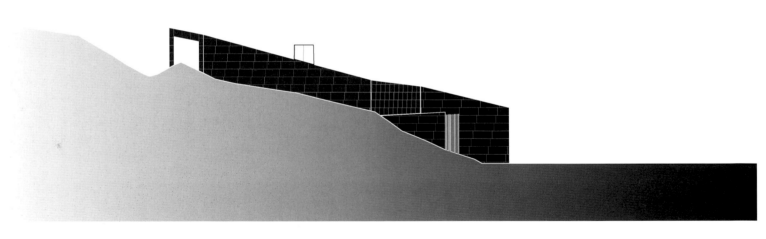

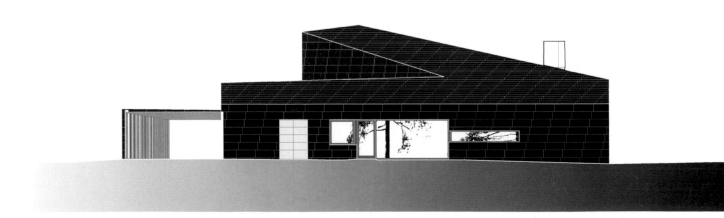

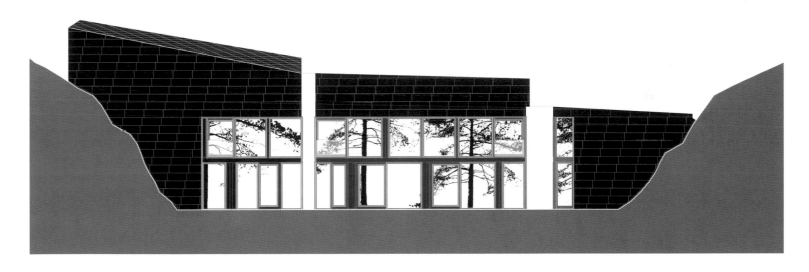

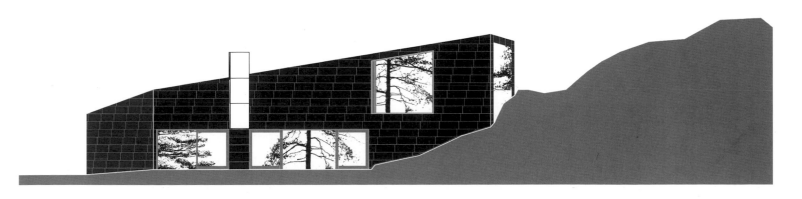

The structure of the house makes it completely waterproof without any incorporated organic materials. Copper ions from the façade can be neutralized by crushed limestone along the plinth.

ELINE STRIJKERS

Unit 9

Amsterdam, The Netherlands   *Photographs: Teo Krijgsman*

The floor plan nearly always provides the basis for the organization of functions; when a dwelling is organized vertically, using a multistory elevation as the point of departure, the result can have a completely different character. In this particular dwelling-cum-workplace the functions are connected to the walls and not to the floors.

This is how the existing shell of a harbor building (measuring some 2691 sq ft or 250 sqm) in Amsterdam-North has been approached. All supporting functions are enclosed volumes. Because work, storage, seating, eating, cooking, and sleeping are all components of a particular volume or surface, the space is almost entirely free of free-standing pieces of furniture.

The volumes unfold like independent sculptures, while at the same time making a free division of the space possible. Here, also, a vertical organization of the space is emphasized. There is a clear division between the ground floor and the other levels, which have been handled as a spatial whole.

The radical nature of the spatial concept lies mainly in the way that Strijkers has developed the unexpected materialization of her design, down to the smallest detail. At ground level, a different material was used to create transitions from one room to another.

The materials used upstairs give terms like 'domesticity' and ' coziness' an entirely new frame of reference. Despite all the attention paid to space, form, materials and details, the rooms are not ruined by a profusion of design. The prevailing casual atmosphere is the result of an unpolished use of materials, a sense of openness between the various parts of this home/workspace and, in particular, the tendency toward collective use.

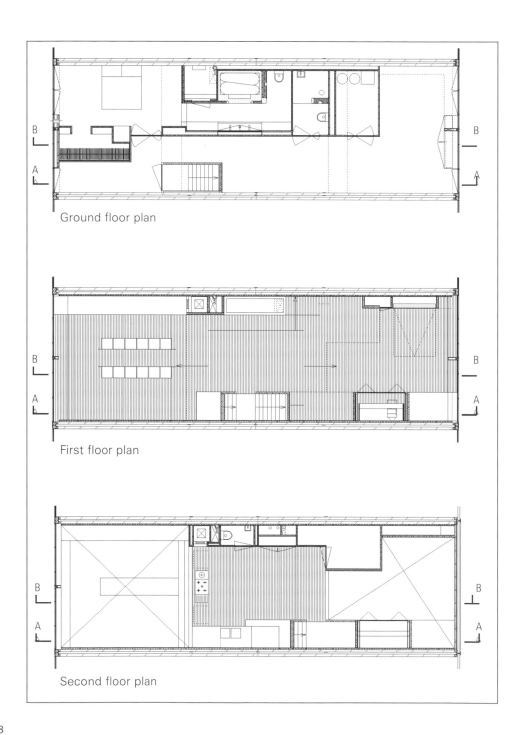

Ground floor plan

First floor plan

Second floor plan

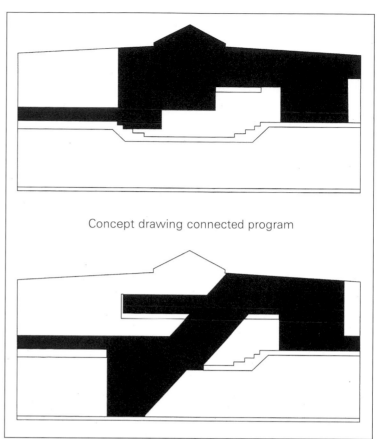

Concept drawing connected program

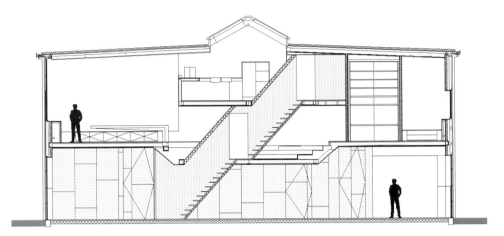

Section AA

The radical nature of this apartment's spatial concept lies in the way that the functions are directly connected to the walls rather than to the floor space.

The work, storage, seating, eating, cooking and sleeping functions are all components of a particular volume or surface, the space is almost entirely devoid of freestanding furniture.

Section BB

HIROAKI OHTANI

Layer House

Kobe, Japan

Photographs: Kouji Okamoto

The architect chose a very small plot measuring only 355.21 sq ft (33 sq m) in the heart of Kobe city for his family home. The challenge (and central design theme) was to create as spacious and rich an indoor space as possible on such a tiny plot bounded by existing buildings at the back and sides. Since such restraints also meant that large construction equipment could not be used, the architect came up with a new construction method, in which pre-stressed concrete strips were manually stacked to form the walls; the construction is thus entirely devoid of vertical members. Being custom designed by the eventual inhabitants of the home, the design scheme incorporates their own very personal preferences and philosophies. For example, they wanted a house that would be open toward the city while at the same time maintaining a sense of privacy. Hence, the front façade of the house is largely glazed, yet the floors have been placed above or below the level of the street to eliminate direct sight lines. In spite of the site's highly reduced proportions, the architect made the unconventional decision to set the façade back from the edge of the plot in order to make room to plant a tall tree just outside the windows of the front façade. Inside, care has been taken to ensure fluidity - not a single space has stagnant air. This has been achieved, in part, through the lack of partitions on each floor. This also creates a greater sense of space, as do the continuous connections between the floors; the cantilevered steps of these gentle flights of stairs become pieces of furniture in the rooms where they originate.

The decision to include very little storage space was deliberate - this way the occupants are immediately faced with messes and are thereby prompted to keep the spaces tidy. The few storage spaces and bookshelves that have been deemed necessary are all elevated so that every corner of the floor surface is visible, thus ensuring greater visual spaciousness. The pervading sense of order in this house is heightened by the effective concealing of light switches and receptacles, such as, for example, between the pre-cast wall elements. None of the lighting fixtures and shelves, even those that have been inserted into the voids in the walls, is fixed; they can all be quickly and easily relocated.

The pre-cast concrete wall elements are not completely uniform in size and shape and many of them have minor cracks or are chipped. These irregularities were embraced as an important part of the overall look of the home; the architect views them as examples of "beautiful variety".

Site plan

Since large construction equipment could not be used, the architect came up with a new construction method, in which pre-stressed concrete strips were manually stacked to form the walls. Pre-cast concrete wall elements are not completely uniform in size and shape and many of them have minor cracks or are chipped. These irregularities were embraced as an important part of the overall look of the home; the architect views them as examples of "beautiful variety".

West elevation

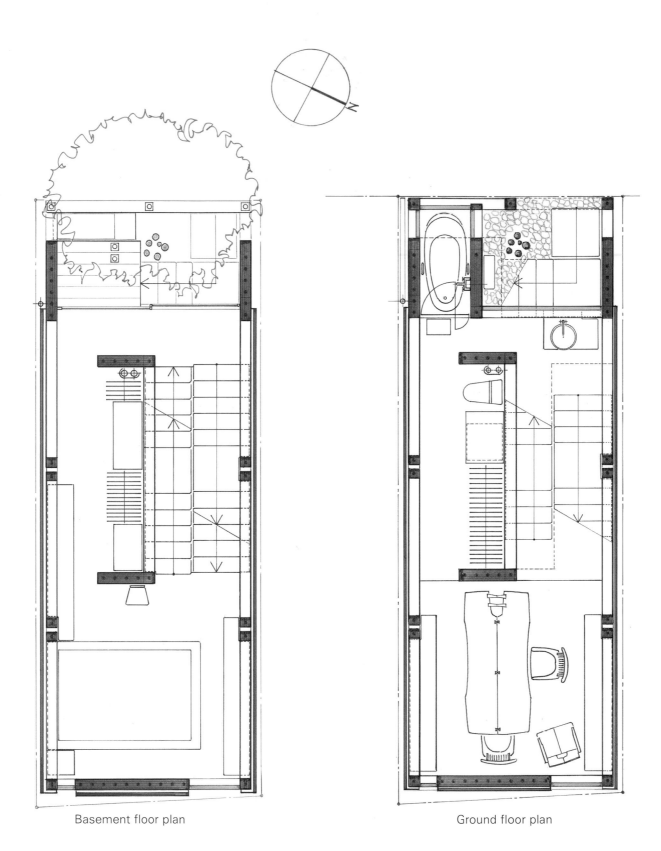

Basement floor plan

Ground floor plan

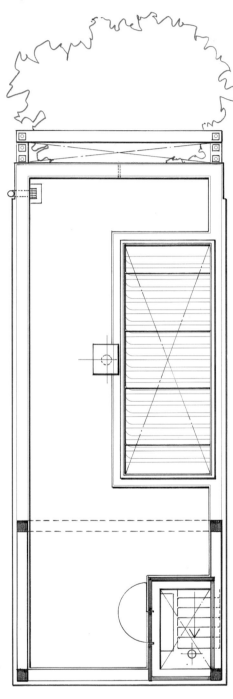

First floor plan

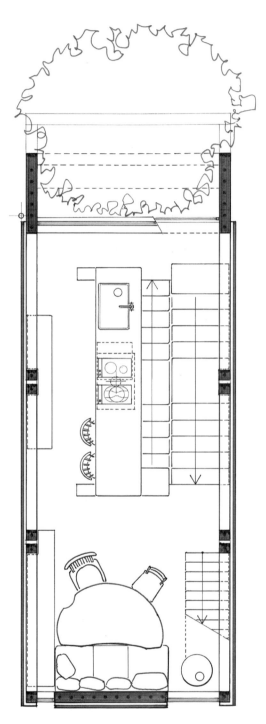

Roof plan

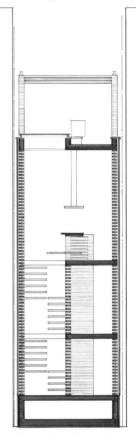

South North section

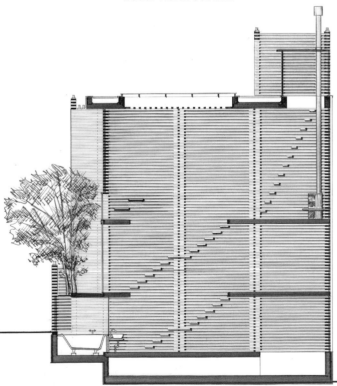

East West section

RECDI8

Loft in Poble Sec

Barcelona, Spain

Photographs: Lane de Castro

The project called for the conversion of a defunct woodworking shop, located on a ground floor measuring 1076.39 sqft (100 sqm) with a ceiling height of 14.76 ft (4.5 sqm), into a comfortable habitable space. The floor plan is divided into two main parts joined by a completely white Zen-inspired space. The entire length of the apartment is marked by an interplay of double-height spaces, changes in floor level and lofts. The entryway is located in the building's communal stairwell; this entrance zone organizes the space so that it communicates directly with a small closet, toilet and the dining room. The former entrance to the woodworking shop is also located here and the old wooden doors have been conserved, protected by a double door of steel and acid-etched glass that conceals views from the street.

It is here that the 15 foot ceiling height is divided into two spaces via a loft that supports an office and guestroom concealed by teak wood screens. The kitchen is located beneath this loft and the floor had to be lowered in order to achieve the required height. The thick existing stone wall is the unifying element between these two zones. Here, the lighting is provided by fixtures set into the floor.

The flooring is in resin in almost the entire apartment, except for the slate paving in the master bedroom and the oil-treated pine parquet of the guestroom.

On the wall opposite the kitchen is a combination bench/storage unit with a retro look created by the interplay of the wood's color, a reflective gold enameled tiling and lighting fixtures affixed to the wall.

The kitchen gives way to a space finished entirely in white, where soft light is filtered through a skylight in the central zone that was once used as the building's ventilation shaft but which now features a steel and acid-etched glass ceiling and small points of light lying almost flush with the ground. Here also, two stylized windows cast natural light into the main bathroom.

Past this zone, the apartment again opens up into a space with a ceiling at the same height as the first. This space has been split into three areas. First is the TV room, with two '70s-style armchairs and an entertainment unit containing the TV, stereo, CDs, DVD and a bar. A short flight of stairs leads to the first shift in level, where there is a living room overlooking the courtyard on the other side. Here, the openings of the original space have been conserved, and ample light floods this zone. Finally, the master bedroom is set alongside the living room on a platform paved in slate and partially lit by natural light filtering through teak wood screens. The same untreated pine that is used in the other storage units in the house has also been used for the master bedroom closet. A restored antique marble sink now graces the main bathroom, which has been painted in gray stucco for a colder, more industrial feel.

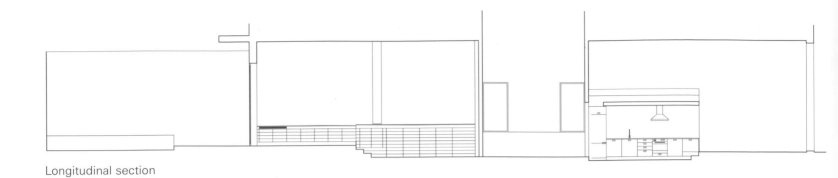

Longitudinal section

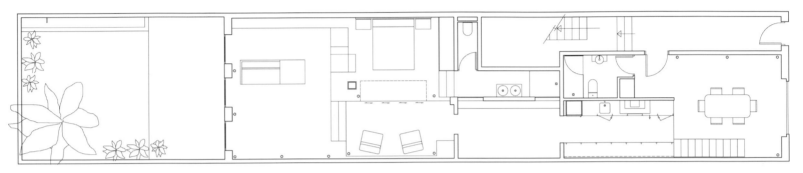

Floor plan

Finally, the master bedroom is set alongside the living room on a platform paved in slate and partially lit by natural light filtering through teak wood screens. A restored antique marble sink now graces the main bathroom, which has been painted in gray stucco for a colder, more industrial feel.

CARLO DONATI

Loft A

Milan, Italy   *Photographs: Matteo Piazza*

Loft A is located in a typical banister house in the centre of Milan. It is the result of the unification of three different units. Actually the loft was subdivided in two small flats, one on the ground floor one on the first floor, linked by a long passage to a recently built block, a wide art gallery.

The connection of these three units which differed in their characteristics, was to produce a major architectural challenge.

The first projectual step consisted of defining the connection between the three separate units.

The old, long and blind passage at the entrance was transformed into a double egg-shaped volume, two pure bodies inserted one into the other following axis with different directions.

The helicoidal stairs lead from the first oval to the bedrooms of the upper floor.

The access to the main bedroom is in the second oval, this area is completely independent, with a wide bathroom, wardrobe, and direct access to the private inner garden.

The rooms on the ground floor weave in and out of each like characters in a story. Entering the kitchen it is possible to understand the arrangement of the living area, whose spaces rotate around the interior garden, which is the pivot of the whole apartment.

The living room is an open space where the dining, home theatre, fireplace and conversation area are in sequence. The route is completed by a small swimming pool, on which the mezzanine-study faces (related to a relaxation area, a sauna, a shower and a bathroom) scenographically projected like part of the living, just separated by huge fixed glasses from the rest of the space.

The architectural choices were supported by innovative materials and avant-garde technical solutions. Corian was used for the furniture, while the woods are refined and unusual essences, the floors are all made of resins.

The technical solutions involved the use of carbon fibres with structural functions, the heating system was realized with ground radiant panels of the last productive generation. They have the double functions of heating during wintertime, and of refreshing and de-humidifying during summertime.

The lighting plant is innovative and guarantees maximum flexibility in lighting and the automation of all home - equipment via remote control, personal computer or mobile phone.

The old, long and blind passage at the entrance was transformed into a double egg-shaped volume, two pure bodies inserted one into the other following axis with different directions.

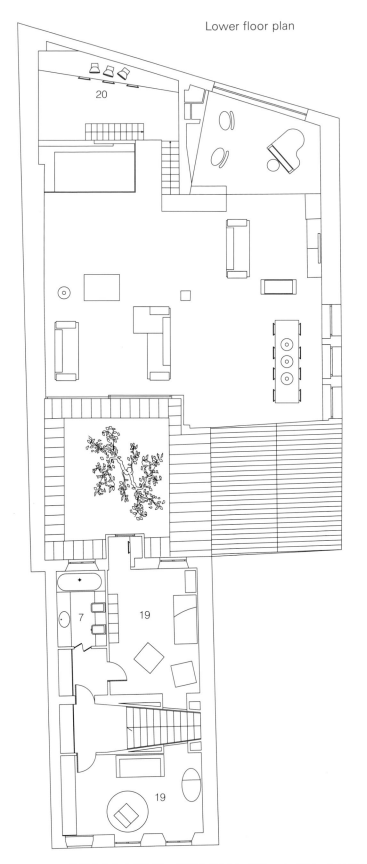

Lower floor plan

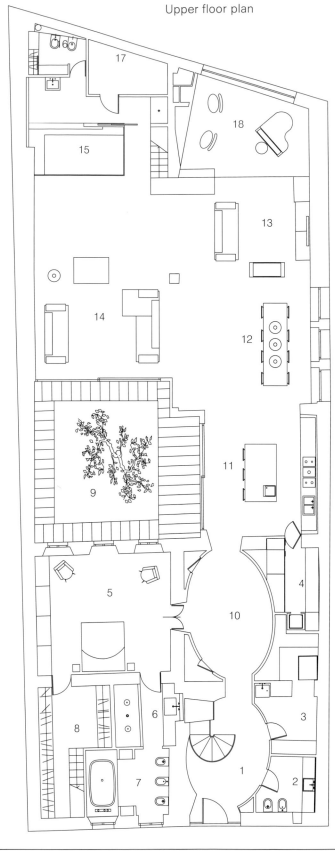

Upper floor plan

1. Oval hall	5. Parents bedroom	9. Garden	13. T.V. room	17. Sauna
2. Guest bathroom	6. Bathroom	10. Oval distribution space	14. Living room	18. Relaxation
3. Service	7. Bathroom	11. Kitchen	15. Swimming pool	19. Children's bedroom
4. Pantry	8. Closet	12. Dining room	16. Pool area bathroom	20. Study

The lighting plant is innovative and guarantees maximum flexibility in lighting and the automation of all home - equipment via remote control, personal computer or mobile phone.

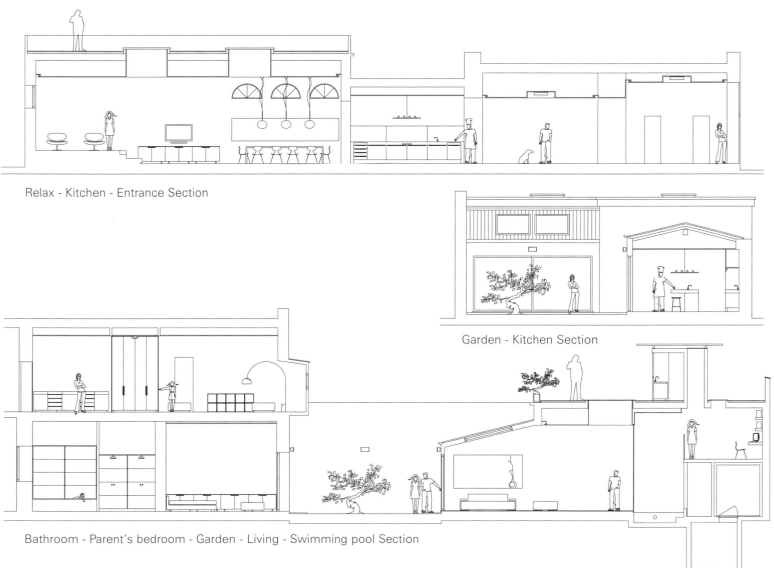

Relax - Kitchen - Entrance Section

Garden - Kitchen Section

Bathroom - Parent's bedroom - Garden - Living - Swimming pool Section

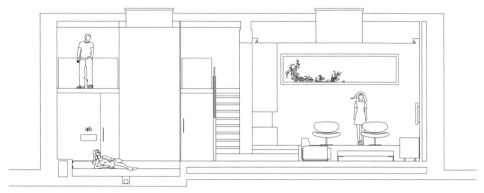

Swimming pool - Living Section

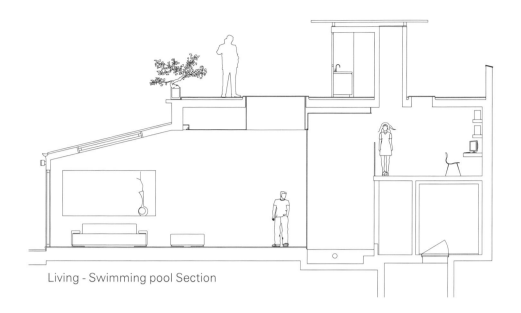

Living - Swimming pool Section

JOHNSON CHOU

Womb: Work, Office, Meditation, Base

Toronto, Canada

Photographs: Filippo Vinardi

'Retreat' invokes more than escape - we retreat to contemplate, reflect and create, to harness the creativity and focus we sometimes lack. It is where we physically and intellectually rejuvenate, a place where books are written, design concepts formed - where one is creatively inspired.

A multi-functional (home/office) space, Womb (for work, office, meditation, base), recognizes that our refuge must fulfill a variety of needs. Designed to be four rooms in one, the space transforms as desired, maintaining an elementally ethereal aesthetic.

With furniture and cabinetry that pivot and disappear into walls and floors with a touch of a button, Womb offers four programmatic rooms that occupy the entire 600sqft (56m2) space; kitchen/dining, work/office, bedroom/living, spa/bath, all within a spare, Zen-like meditative environment. Womb proposes a 21st century 'machine for living' - concealing what isn't immediately necessary, eliminating visual distractions and quadrupling its spatial effectiveness.

The kitchen unit slides into the wall when not needed, and the empty space allows a table to pivot around, a clean work area with an unobstructed view across the pool to the exterior. Sink and work surfaces are hidden under covers that open to an upright position. In the center of the room, the bathing/reflecting pool and suspended stainless steel fireplace anchor the space as the only fixed elements.

Expanding and contracting as needed, the washroom is situated centrally near the pool and fireplace. A "u"-shaped wall that conceals the bathroom slides to allow one to enter, or to enclose the occupant for privacy. When not in use, the wall automatically closes, completely regaining the space. The living area, separated by the pool from the work/kitchen space, contains a bed that disappears into the floor when not required, allowing a cantilevered couch to fold out from the wall.

The walls are a blank canvas for lighting to transform, fluorescents creating a cool white daytime space that recessed halogen lights turn to a warmer intimacy by evening. Further modulation is achieved with fiber-optics that "paint" the walls with variable hues.

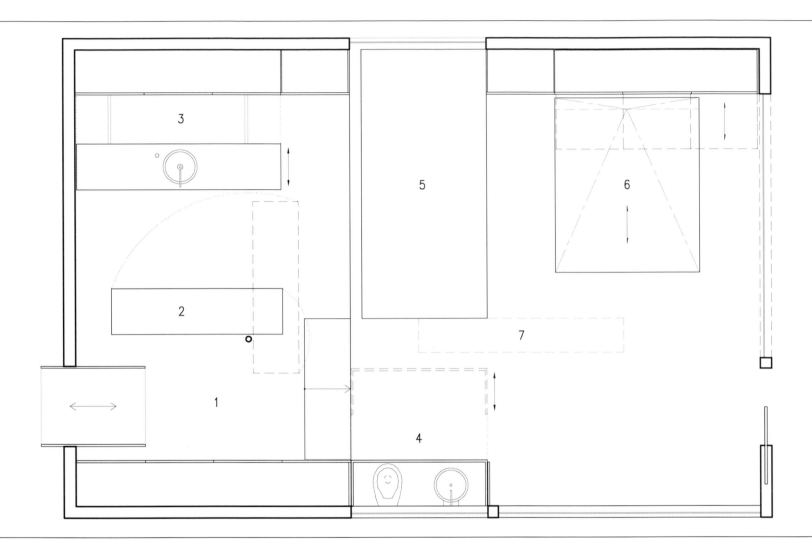

1. Foyer
2. Pivoting table
3. Retractable kitchen
4. Bathroom
5. Whirlpool/bath
6. Bedroom
7. Fireplace

Animated by the ballet movements of the architectural elements, bathed in nuances of light, this is an environment designed to inspire reflection, creation and contemplation yet able to transform itself for living purposes. Womb is truly a base for work, office and meditation.